# Teaching
## and Leading

## From the Inside Out

*He who looks outside*

*Dreams*

*He who looks inside*

*Awakens*

— Carl Jung

# *Teaching*
## and *Leading*

## From the Inside Out

A Model for Reflection,
Exploration,
and Action

Judy F. Carr
Janice R. Fauske
Stephen Rushton

**CORWIN PRESS**
A SAGE Company
Thousand Oaks, CA 91320

*For information:*

Corwin Press, Inc.
A SAGE Company
2455 Teller Road
Thousand Oaks, California 91320
E-mail: order@corwinpress.com

SAGE India Pvt. Ltd.
M-32 Market
Greater Kailash I
New Delhi 110 048 India

SAGE Ltd.
6 Bonhill Street
London EC2A 4PU
United Kingdom

SAGE Asia-Pacific Pte. Ltd.
33 Pekin Street #02-01
Far East Square
Singapore 048763

Printed in the United States of America

*Library of Congress Cataloging-in-Publication Data*

Carr, Judy F.
Teaching and leading from the inside out: a model for reflection, exploration, and action / Judy F. Carr, Janice R. Fauske, Stephen Rushton.
    p. cm.
Includes bibliographical references.
ISBN 978-1-4129-2666-9 (cloth) — ISBN 978-1-4129-2667-6 (pbk.)
    1. Reflective teaching. 2. Teachers—Professional relationships. I. Fauske, Janice R.    II. Rushton, Stephen.    III. Title..

LB1025 3 C386 2008
371.9—dc22                           2007040306

This book is printed on acid-free paper.

08   09   10   11   10   9   8   7   6   5   4   3   2   1

| | |
|---|---|
| *Acquisitions Editor:* | Rachel Livsey |
| *Managing Editor:* | Debra Stollenwerk |
| *Editorial Assistants:* | Jordan Barbakow, Allison Scott |
| *Production Editor:* | Appingo Publishing Services |
| *Cover Designer:* | Lisa Riley |

# Contents

# Preface

*Teaching and Leading From the Inside Out* presents a comprehensive model of individual and collective professional reflection, exploration, and action. This book also includes associated tools that educators can use to implement individual, team, department, and schoolwide systems honoring the recursive relationships among the personal and professional aspects of teaching and leading. *Personal* refers to who we are as people and as teachers and leaders. *Professional* has to do with theories, publications, and policies; professional organizations; and formal learning opportunities that inform and guide practice, as well as with what each teacher and leader offers to the profession in return.

The book is organized around the three essential concepts of authenticity, agency, and appreciation:

- **Authenticity.** Matching one's inner being with one's outer actions in all that one does.
- **Agency.** Acting from a place of inner conviction and confidence in one's self.
- **Appreciation.** Focusing on one's positive attributes and efforts, and celebrating individual and collective accomplishments.

These elements are explored from the perspective of teachers who are often informal leaders in their schools as well as from the perspective of school administrators who are also teachers and learners. Thus the terms *teachers* and *leaders* are used throughout this book as inclusive rather than mutually exclusive terms.

The book is based on synthesis of the work of educator's such as Parker Palmer, Elliot Eisner, Stephen Covey, Donald Schon, Richard DuFour, Roland Barth, Michael Fullan, Michael Apple, and James Bean. The authors' long-term work with schools, state agencies, foundations, and community organizations provides a rich context for development of the content in ways that make it directly applicable in school settings. Cases and vignettes are used to illustrate key points, and these include, in italics throughout the book, illustrative stories from the authors' own experiences. Suggested engagements involving reflection, exploration, and action are included at the end of each chapter to engage practitioners in reflecting and making the book's key concepts their own.

Judy Carr
Janice Fauske
Stephen Rushton
Sarasota, Florida
May 2007

# Acknowledgments

By way of illustration, we have included in italics throughout this book vignettes and examples that come from our own experiences as students, as teachers, and as leaders. We are grateful to the many individuals—teachers, administrators, students, parents, colleagues, mentors and coaches, friends, siblings, children—who have contributed to each of us, the three authors, becoming more aware of our own "inside outness."

We are deeply appreciative of the pioneering work of Parker Palmer to engage teachers and school leaders in community processes to examine their lives and their work. Similarly, our decision to incorporate our own stories in support of essential points was influenced in significant ways by the writing of Robert Nash on scholarly personal narrative. Thanks, too, to Ken Bergstrom for his demonstration, personal and professional, of a deep commitment to authenticity, agency, and appreciation.

The idea for this book took root in a chance conversation with Rachel Livsey at Corwin Press. We wish to thank her for her ongoing support throughout the process of writing. Thank you, too, to Debra Stollenwerk for her help in bringing this book to publication.

Corwin Press wishes to thank the following reviewers for their editorial insight and guidance:

Mary Beth Cunat
Director, Principal Professional Development
Chicago Public Schools
Chicago, Illinois

Sheila R. Cole
Principal
Franklin Elementary School
Summit, New Jersey

Jennifer York-Barr
Professor
Educational Policy and Administration
University of Minnesota
Minneapolis, Minnesota

Julie Moore
Lower School Facilitator, Third-Grade Teacher
B'nai Shalom Day School
Greensboro, North Carolina

Karl H. Clauset
Consultant
Clauset Consulting
Bellingham, Washington

Kathy Malnar
Superintendent
Hudson Area Schools
Hudson, Michigan

# About the Authors

**Judy F. Carr** teaches half-time in the Educational Leadership Program at the University of South Florida Sarasota-Manatee. She is also Codirector of the Center for Curriculum Renewal, working as a consultant, facilitator, professional development specialist, workshop presenter and program evaluator with educators and policymakers in the United States, Canada, and the Caribbean. She is coauthor or coeditor of the following books:

- *A Pig Don't Get Fatter the More You Weigh It: Balancing Classroom Assessment*
- *Creating Dynamic Schools Through Mentoring, Coaching, and Collaboration*
- *Succeeding with Standards: Linking Curriculum, Assessment, and Action Planning*
- *How to Use Standards in the Classroom*
- *Integrated Studies in the Middle Grades: Dancing Through Walls*
- *Living and Learning in the Middle Grades: The Dance Continues: A Festschrift for Chris Stevenson*

Judy Carr has expertise in K–12 curriculum, instruction, and assessment; standards-based education reform; design of professional development materials and processes; systems change implementation with leadership teams in school districts and state agencies; and middle grades education. She has been a middle school teacher and a K-12 curriculum director. She was the recipient of the second annual Vermont ASCD Curriculum Leadership Award.

### Janice R. Fauske

Upon earning a B.A. in English with secondary teaching endorsement, Janice Fauske began her career as a seventh grade English teacher in a rural, economically deprived school district in Virginia. After earning an M.S. Ed. in Reading Psychology, she taught special education in an inner city school district and later began teaching at a small Virginia college. She earned an Educational Specialist degree in Higher Education at College of William and Mary, and later completed her Ph.D. in Educational Administration at the University of Utah. Before joining the University of South Florida faculty as associate professor in Educational Leadership and Policy Studies, Dr. Fauske worked as the Assistant Commissioner for Academic Affairs at the Utah State Board of Regents, as a faculty member and administrator at Weber State University, as founding Dean of the School of Education at Westminster College, and associate professor and Doctoral Advisor in Educational Leadership and Policy at the University of Utah.

Janice's teaching expertise includes methods of teaching and learning for school leaders, leadership, organizational change, and qualitative research methods. Research interests include organizational learning and change, effects of collaborative governance on teaching and learning in schools, and teaching in educational administration programs. Recent publications include "Collaboration to Strengthen Classroom Assessment," in P. Jones, R. Ataya, and J. Carr (Eds.), *A Pig Don't Get Fatter the More You Weigh It: Balancing Assessment for the Classroom;* "Organizational Theory in Schools" in the *Journal of Educational Administration,* and "Theories of Collaboration in Education" in the *Encyclopedia of Educational Leadership and Administration.*

## Stephen Rushton

Stephen Rushton is an Associate Professor in the Childhood Education Department at the University of South Florida Sarasota-Manatee, and he has been teaching for USF for the last eight years. He supervises student teachers and teaches courses in research, elementary education methods, and the writing process. Dr. Rushton previously taught elementary education for twelve years in Ontario, Canada, and Oakridge, Tennessee. He conducts research on teacher effectiveness, brain research, and personality types using the Myers-Briggs Personality Inventory. He received his B.Sc. and B.Ed. from Queen's University in Canada and his M.S. and Ph.D. from the University of Tennessee and is presently the Coordinator for the Masters of Arts in Teaching program.

# 1

# Teaching and Leading From the Inside Out

CHAPTER CONTENTS

Each of us attempts to make sense of who we are as educators. In our lives as teachers and leaders, we incorporate who we are on the inside—our nature and needs, experiences and perceptions—with the outside demands of our students and our colleagues, with the roles and responsibilities we are assigned explicitly by superiors and the school board or implicitly by state and national policies, and with the recommendations of professional organizations. Often it is the outside expectations that take precedence, and the selves we bring to our work recede. In that process, we sometimes lose significant opportunities for professional growth along with vital possibilities to influence our professional environment and the lives of the students, colleagues, and peers who are there to learn and grow, as well.

We teach and lead based largely on how we have experienced teaching and leadership in our own lives as students. We may emulate the ninth-grade French teacher who taught us to believe in ourselves or the elementary school principal who honored our success on spelling tests by delivering in person a shiny, blue pencil engraved with the school's name. Often our view is shaped by the examples we see, but sometimes we create structures for how we teach and lead based on how different we wish to be from those who educated us. For example, we might avoid emulating a teacher for whom we completed countless "busy work" worksheets or who required us to memorize passages from textbooks. We might intentionally develop skills to avoid treating others badly to avoid the ways others have treated us in the past.

*I was teaching language arts in a middle school when a new language arts coordinator was hired for the school. He had expertise in writing as a process, and he was highly regarded for workshops and courses he had conducted on that topic. Soon after he was hired, it became evident he was not as highly skilled in administrative skills. Meetings were held without agendas, and no minutes were kept. New programs were imposed without discussion. He would share indiscreetly with other teachers what he had seen in classrooms of teachers he'd visited for formal observations. Morale declined very quickly. When I became a curriculum director in a different district, my clarity about the importance of confidentiality and trust, about ground rules and good processes for meetings, and about engagement of teachers in decisions that would impact them helped both the teachers and me to be successful in implementing some major changes in the curriculum without undermining morale.*

Humans learn and remember by connecting new ideas to existing structures built from previous knowledge and experience (Piaget, 1926; Ausubel, 1967; Gagne & Driscoll, 1988). Suppose you overheard the following conversation between two high school friends:

A:  What did you get?
B:  My parents are going to be so mad!
A:  You didn't do so well, huh?

Do you know what the classmates are talking about? Chances are you're pretty sure they are discussing recent grades they received. But how can you know this? You know this based on your own schema developed from having received grades in school.

Similarly, teachers and leaders each have a schema for what teaching and leading look like in schools, and this schema is shaped by a relatively narrow range of experiences. Many teachers and school leaders have developed schema based on experiences in a particular contextual setting and have rarely worked in more than one or two schools or districts. Such experience can lead us to develop a limited "response set" (Woolfolk, 1993) based on what has worked in the past, but these same strategies may not work in a different or changing environment. Many of the vastly larger array of approaches that positively impact the experiences and results of students in grades K–12 remain outside our awareness, but when we expand our response sets related to schools and schooling through reading and research and interactions with colleagues from other schools and districts, we much more readily think outside the limiting school "lunch box."

Although the meanings we make of events in our lives can be limited by our current range of understanding (Wheatley,

1994), we still can learn from carefully considering and reflecting on our experiences. The reflective practitioner thinks about what he or she is doing (reflection in action) and what he or she has done (reflection on action) in the classroom or school (Schon, 1983). Reflective teachers and leaders continually revisit their reasons for doing the work they do, the connections between this work and their lives outside of work, and the meaning they make of these connections (Palmer, 1998). When we have diverse avenues, tools, processes, and experiences to help contextualize and reexamine how we interpret what is going on around us, the understanding of our motives, intentions, and actions is more solid, grounded, and honest.

## FROM INSIDE TO OUTSIDE: THE PERSONAL PROFESSIONAL CONTINUUM

The metaphor "inside out" denotes two simultaneous perspectives operating together yet separately, parallel yet juxtaposed. The move from personal to professional is, in essence, the move from the inside to the outside of one's professional being. It provides an image for exploring how we perceive ourselves internally, how we interact with others, and how we are influenced by and connected to the external realities of the profession we have chosen. The self as teacher and leader exists independently, yet also interdependently with the outside world, bringing our inner selves (our guiding beliefs, assumptions, emotions, and values) to the norms for behavior in three dimensions: authenticity, agency, and appreciation. Examining those dimensions provides the opportunity to reassess, refine, and integrate the various representations and interpretations we have of ourselves in relationship to others in our own settings and in relation to the larger professional context.

In reflecting on these dimensions, it is helpful to spend time thinking about questions such as the following:

- ■ What does it mean to me to be authentic in my work? In my personal life? In my interactions with colleagues?

**Figure 1.1**  Dimensions of Teaching and Leading from the Inside Out

| INSIDE | | |
|---|---|---|
| | **Personal** | **Professional** |
| **Authenticity** | *Personal (inward) Authenticity* requires an honest, introspective awareness of self with continual self-improvement (from the inside) and a commitment to making sense of one's professional activities in context (from the outside). It necessitates genuine engagement with collaborative others as well as open exploration of ideas and alternatives and includes the ability to see yourself as others see you. | *Professional Authenticity* entails passion and commitment for maintaining currency and skill in one's professional endeavors while honoring others and context. It includes the ability to act with respect for others' positions while remaining open to alternative views. |
| **Agency** | *Personal Agency* is the use of one's internal sense of power that flows from these dimensions and is the ability and choice to act from an informed and moral perspective as a dimension of self actualization. | *Professional Agency* emerges from personal agency in robust, empathetic advocacy for those ideals that promote the well-being and success of students and fellow educators. It emerges from considerations for social justice, quality, and informed decision making with efforts to improve the profession through development of sound policy structures and new theories of practice and action. |
| **Appreciation** | *Personal Appreciation* involves acknowledging and celebrating one's own accomplishments in a context of caring. It includes recognizing one's strengths and nurturing those strengths. | *Professional Appreciation* entails celebration of collective success, mutual development of materials and learnings, and organized approaches to recognizing the value of working together with colleagues. It includes sharing one's professional work beyond one's own school through publishing and presenting at regional, state, and national conferences. In this way, we join the collective professional conversation and celebrate both small and large accomplishments and victories. |
| | | **OUTSIDE** |

- Do I bring my best self to my work? Does my work nurture the continuing evolution of who I am and wish to be?
- What brought me into this profession? Is this where I am meant to be?
- How do I benefit from working with colleagues? What do I offer to them?
- When did I first experience my own sense of agency? How has it been nurtured? In what ways might I strengthen it?
- What opportunities have I had to hear the appreciation others have for my work? In what ways do I celebrate my own accomplishments? Those of my colleagues or students? Those of my team, department, school, or district?

## AUTHENTICITY

Authenticity means being true to oneself, honoring one's strengths and needs, and understanding the importance of one's history while remaining open to the possibilities of one's future. Personal authenticity emerges from continual self-awareness as we change and grow professionally, and reflecting on that knowledge of self can lead us to different choices and alternate professional journeys, as is illustrated in the following reflection:

> Growing up I had been excited about becoming an urban plan-
> ner. I was in my final semester, about to graduate with a joint
> major in psychology and urban planning, as I was going to save
> the world and plan cities in which people could live together
> more peacefully. Then one day, an event occurred that com-
> pletely changed the course of my life and career.
>
> The mother of a friend said, "I have a surprise for you, but I
> can't tell you what it is. Are you willing to meet me on Monday
> morning at 8:40 and I'll take you some place?" Of course I said,
> "Yes," as I loved surprises then and still do.

*Monday morning arrived and she quietly drove to Queen Victoria Public School. As we pulled up, I wondered what the surprise was as I hadn't been in a public school since I was public-school age. She told me to go to room 12 and introduce myself to the second-grade teacher. And so I did.*

*The teacher welcomed me into her classroom, smiled, and asked me to take a seat. I could barely fit in the chair! As the class began, a funny thing occurred: I sat mesmerized, listening, wondering, wanting something; and then it happened. A palpable sensation swept though my entire body and I knew in an instant that I was to devote my life to work with children and teachers.*

Each of us has our own reasons for becoming a teacher or school leader. For some, the purpose relates to economic concerns, with little regard for the "fit" between the self and the job. For others, the journey to the new credential is, in and of itself, an exploration of personal, collegial, and professional self. Often, the choice of education as a career is based on a genuine desire to serve, to make a difference in the lives of children. This genuine commitment to serve is at the heart of professional authenticity, and it flourishes best in an atmosphere of mutual trust and respect.

Have you ever walked into a school building where everything looked "perfect?" Students' writing is displayed on the wall, colorful pictures and images abound, and yet you have a clear sense that, "Something doesn't quite add up here." Upon closer examination, all of the students' writing assignments are identical, and several classrooms display the exact same assignment completed on the same day. The uniformity of both format and content is immediately apparent. Hallways and classrooms are quiet. Students' desks are in rows, and, in every classroom you pass, students sit working independently. The school culture exudes a certain pressure that beckons teachers and students to obey, to be "good citizens," and not to disturb the status quo. Such a school culture is indicative of the absence of the authentic self and inhibits mutual participation as authentic colleagues. Professional authenticity cannot flourish, and individuals are reluctant to expose their inner selves in such an environment.

On the other hand, imagine a school where children are hanging their own art in the hallway, and teachers and parents work shoulder to shoulder in the classrooms. The principal is rarely behind her desk because she visits classrooms. Walking by the open doors of classrooms reveals students huddled in groups on the floor reading to each other, gathered around a table chattering over a science experiment, or singing softly as they transition from math to social studies. Teachers often switch classrooms or combine classes to share resources and experiment with new teaching ideas. The culture of the school is inviting to people and their ideas. Taking risks, sharing, and even making mistakes are expected parts of the cultural fabric that encourages mutually authentic colleagues. Professional authenticity can flourish when individuals and groups take thoughtful and creative risks. The inner self is more readily revealed in an environment of creativity and mutual trust.

In an environment of mutual respect and shared learning, authentic professionals are committed to keeping current in the field and passionately pursuing questions about content, pedagogy, communication, and leadership approaches. Genuine commitment to and engagement in being the best professional self requires authentically becoming a learner in a community of learners. Being a learner similarly requires that we admit to not having all the answers ourselves. It involves understanding that knowledge and meaning are con-structed from synthesis of information, reflection on one's own experience, observation of good practice, and dialogue with other knowledgeable professionals. Many educators feel compelled to present information as fact, to give answers rather than to ask questions. Yet some of the world's greatest scientists are those who freely admit to not having the answers, who acknowledge that many of their hypotheses have been incorrect. Being professionally authentic means asking a question for which one has not yet discovered an answer and trusting that the answer lies within us.

In the world of K–12 education, professional authenticity has seed in the ongoing dialogue about teaching and learning that occurs among teachers and school leaders. In schools, educators have regular exchanges of information through established teams or committees. They often have a "voice" in both school and grade-level decision making. When such dialogue is routine rather than an exception, teachers and leaders are able to be professionally authentic, moving beyond their individual duties and concerns to collectively govern, make decisions, and influence in multiple ways the learning of their students across the school.

## AGENCY

When we make individual choices about how to address an issue or concern, we exercise personal agency and become agents of change. Each of us has a guiding philosophy that is shaped by beliefs and experiences. Recognizing and articulating that philosophy leads us into making reasoned and thoughtful professional choices favoring one teaching method over another, one text over another, or one leadership style over another. It is in the process of acting on these choices that our personal agency emerges. A well-developed and refined guiding philosophy can enable the making of sound educational decisions and can help us inform others' decision and actions. We can see the potential for personal agency as we consider our many educational choices, the decisions that we can influence, and the benefit that we can bring to schools and students.

*As a reading specialist, I served on several committees that were charged with making decisions about textbooks and related instructional materials. In my role on the textbook-selection committees for departments, I often conducted readability tests on the favored textbooks. I also examined the textbooks carefully for organizational aids and study guides or activities. Although I prefer that teachers not rely solely on texts, I knew that many used the texts as the primary, if not the only, instructional tool. If I could influence text selection, I could help more students succeed. One history text to be selected for eighth grade, for example, had a readability level of grade nine and presented the text in long passages with few subheadings. When faced with these data, the department decided to choose a much more reader-friendly text with a readability level of 7.5 and to supplement it with additional materials in classes where student needed greater challenges.*

*I was not able to fully enact my strong belief that teachers should not be bound by texts, but I was able to share information important to decision making. Thus, we chose texts that were much more accessible and more teachable to certain students. Both teachers and students could benefit from this decision.*

Advocating a position or approach that is in the best interest of students is easy for most educators. Complications come with disagreement over what is best for students and over who decides. When we advocate a position, decision, or approach in a group setting either with or against other group members, we exercise professional agency. It is the belief that one can truly make a difference that sustains personal agency and leads to self-actualization. Professional agency similarly emerges from our personal beliefs and choices, but is shaped by others' contributions and beliefs, either shared or opposing.

Identification of a problem or issue and working for a solution with others who can collectively influence how resources are allocated and how programs are delivered is an example of *professional agency.*

*In a district-level meeting of all reading specialists, the discussion centered on the need for providing tutors for individual students, particularly at the middle school level when they began changing classes and teachers. Some reading specialists had been drawn into working with individual students rather than with teachers as the role was designed. Some specialists thought that tutoring individual students should be integrated into the role. Others thought that providing individual tutors would perpetuate teachers' tendency to abdicate the responsibility for teaching remedial readers. After much discussion and research, the group unanimously decided on a plan for supervised and assisted study time arranged through parent groups, and peer tutors were arranged at each of the middle schools. A combination of reading, study skills, and test-taking skills was included in the plan. The group advocating that specialists act as tutors, after additional information and discussion, agreed that they might reach more students by focusing on teachers than on individual students. The shared goal of improving student learning allowed the groups to overcome differences and come to a unified decision.*

Professional agency involves putting into action one's authentic personal and professional self, acting on one's commitment to one's profession and to the common good beyond one's own school or classroom.

## APPRECIATION

Personal appreciation encompasses actively acknowledging that you have made a valuable contribution to the students, school, and/or community. Finding the balance between acknowledging one's strengths versus spotlighting one's weaknesses is often difficult, but beginning a change process with a focus on what works can have powerful impacts. Many educators readily focus on their shortcomings and mistakes rather than on their successes, and too often schools are not places where one can openly celebrate one's own accomplishments. Educators typically shy away from perceived self-promotion and recognition, often preferring collective over individual recognition. Realistically and generously examining our own skills and accomplishments is a talent that takes practice, and this process can be encouraged in a school community that places value on regularly recognizing the contributions of its members.

*Years ago when I visited the Junior High of the Kennebunks, I was interested to discover that rather than waiting for a once-a-year student awards ceremony or a one-time teacher of the year recognition banquet, middle school principal Sandra Caldwell instituted a "Friday Letter" that was a compilation of recognition that individuals gave themselves and others. A box was placed in the office and next to it a pile of recognition slips. These could be filled out by anyone who wished to recognize a contribution, small or large, of someone in the school. Every Friday, these were typed up, copied, and posted throughout the school for all to see—a student thanking a janitor for a kind deed, a teacher sharing with others his election to the board of a state organization, or the principal announcing a parent information night sponsored by a local social service agency.*

Professional appreciation involves the ongoing recognition and valuing of the work of colleagues and the school community as a whole. At its best, such recognition becomes a part of the fabric of the school culture and the relationships among professionals in the school or district. Thousands of teachers and leaders belong to national organizations such as the Association for Supervision and Curriculum Development, The National Association of Secondary School Principals, the National Staff Development Council, the National Council of Teachers of Mathematics, and many others. Teachers and leaders play critical roles as well in founding and sustaining state-level organizations. The publications and conferences of these state and national organizations feature articles, books, and conference presentations in which practitioners share and celebrate their own good work.

*When I began my career as a middle school language arts teacher, the curriculum was thematic and skills based. Teachers in the department were in the habit of exchanging folders of materials for each theme at the start of every quarter. The teacher who had taught "Mystery and Suspense" one semester would hand off her folder to whomever was teaching it the next time around, knowing she would receive it back for a future marking period with new material included. After several years, the curriculum changed to feature use of a grammar book and a literature anthology, and sharing of materials stopped. Then, one day, I was leafing through old copies of* Learning *magazine, and I came across an article about teachers publishing their own work. I put the article in the mailboxes of several colleagues with a note asking if anyone would be interested in trying to publish one of our units. One colleague responded in the affirmative, and, over April vacation, we put together a proposal packet that (not knowing any better) we sent to fourteen publishers. We received thirteen rejections and one acceptance!*

Recognizing others' talents and hard work is a hallmark of good teaching and leadership that we too often take for granted rather than approach "planfully" and systematically. Such work can be celebrated as an indicator of moving forward collectively as a profession, the best work of individuals contributing to the improvement of the professional as a whole.

## FOCUS FOR REFLECTION, EXPLORATION, AND ACTION: THE PERSONAL AND PROFESSIONAL TIMELINE

One effective method of initiating the exploration of authenticity, agency, and appreciation of self in relation to colleagues and the profession is to create a personal and professional timeline. Creating such a timeline is a means to consider main events and critical incidents in one's personal life, the opportunities one has had for collegiality and collaboration, and the events in one's professional life and then to look at the connections between the three (Bergstrom, personal communication, 1984). The timelines shown in Figures 1.2, 1.3, and 1.4 demonstrate the different experiences and styles of presentation of those who created them.

**Figure 1.2**   Sample Timeline: Circles

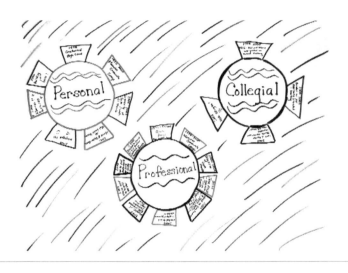

**Figure 1.3**   Sample Timeline: Trees

**Figure 1.4    Sample Timeline: Paths**

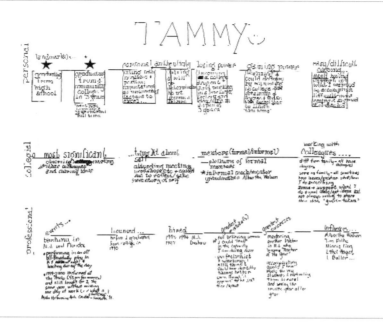

Think about your life from the time when you first considered becoming a teacher. Begin with colored markers and a large sheet of paper; chart paper is ideal for this activity. As you begin to sketch out the key events in your personal life, your collegial relationships, and in your professional life beyond your school, represent these in any way you like, so long as it is possible to see the relationships between the three timelines. You may use words alone or enhance the product with graphic representations and symbols. Some who do this activity choose a very linear approach, while others draw theirs out in free form or more flowing designs. One teacher chose to present hers as two vines on the page, another as three columns created with a computer program, and yet another as sets of lily pads floating on a pond.

As you construct your timelines, consider the following questions, which are designed to promote reflection and help bring to mind those aspects of your personal, collegial, and professional experiences that are of the greatest significance to you at this point in your career.

*Looking Inside Ourselves: Personal*

- What do you consider to be the key "landmarks" in your personal life?
- What has shaped your own sense of personal authenticity?
- What experiences have you had in your life of losing or gaining power?
- What experiences have shaped the ways you celebrate moments of personal significance, for yourself or family members?
- Which parts of your life have been easy and which have been more difficult?
- What events in your life have been most central to the establishment of the sense of yourself you possess today?

*Making Connections with Others: Collegial*

- Which relationships in your life have been most significant?
- Which relationships have taught you the most about yourself?
- Who have been your mentors and coaches, whether formal or informal?
- How is working with colleagues different from or the same as interacting with friends and family members? What examples from your own life illustrate this?

*Looking Outside Ourselves: Professional*

- What events in your life have been most essential in shaping your desire to be a teacher and/or school leader?
- Through what processes and events did you become licensed?
- When were you hired for which jobs?
- What have been some of your greatest mistakes and your greatest successes as an educator?

- Who has influenced your most central beliefs about learning, teaching, and leading?
- What experiences have you had with publishing or presenting your work at conferences, workshops, or courses, whether within your own school and district or beyond in your own state or others?

One teacher who used these questions as a guide produced the sample timeline shown in Figure 1.5.

When the timelines are complete, stand back and compare them. If you choose to complete your timelines on your own, look across the three timelines and pay attention to what you notice about the relationships of one to the others. Does one suggest something you've left out of another? What connections do you notice? Are there similarities or differences in what was going on at various times in your personal, collegial, and professional lives? What notations affirm what you have known about these various aspects of yourself? Are there any surprises?

**Figure 1.5**   Sample Timeline

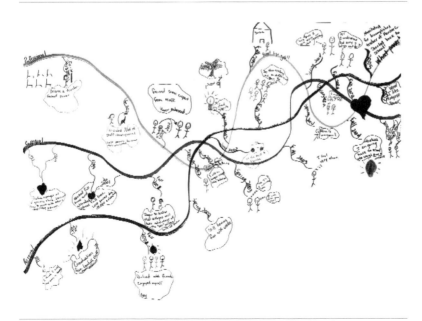

Often, individuals who engage in this process "discover" relationships between their personal, collegial, and professional experiences that they had not previously brought into conscious awareness:

> "Look at that! It was the year after the twins were born that I began work on my master's degree. That certainly was a creative time in my life!"

> "I'd not realized before the extent to which patterns of quiet and activity seem to alternate between my personal and professional lives."

> "I'd not thought before about the extent to which the leadership roles I'd taken on in my church led to my decision to pursue a leadership role in my school."

The creation of the timeline can, in and of itself, provide important "aha's" and new awareness, but the greatest power is in sharing the timelines among colleagues within or across schools. This is an excellent way for new teammates to begin to know each other, for students in a graduate course to expand what they know about themselves and each other, or for two teachers who have worked together for years to deepen their colleagueship and commitment. Very often, it is as one individual explains his or her timelines to others that the full importance of what is represented there becomes clear. Sometimes, when teachers and administrators engage in this activity together in a group setting, it is worthwhile after processing each individual's timelines to identify common themes, as shown in the example in Figure 1.6.

In one group of four in a recent graduate course in the Educational Leadership program, one student explained that when he was diagnosed with cystic fibrosis in early childhood, his parents had been told not to become attached to him because he would not live long. Now thirty-four and a healthy and very highly regarded teacher, he explained his appreciation for their decision to reject that advice and instead embrace him and raise him to be and do whatever he wanted. A second group member spoke of having been born in Cuba, moving to the United States, and then "living between two cultures." A third spoke of how her professional work had sustained her following the death of her three-year-old daughter. The forth and last person to share began by saying, "Compared to all of that, I have nothing to say," but, when encouraged by his peers that his story was of equal value, he shared events that showed how his own experiences growing up in a loving family had helped him create the caring learning environment that characterizes his classroom. It was, in the end, his story that brought all members of the group to tears.

**Figure 1.6**   Identifying Common Themes

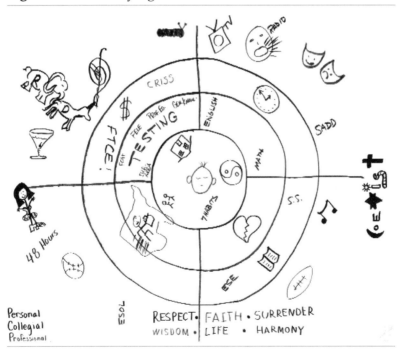

Each individual chooses what to include in the timelines and which events to further elaborate (or not) in the sharing process. One chooses which aspects to "see" or share and which to leave unexplored. For some, this level of sharing personal and professional connections with others is a challenge, but in the challenge is an opportunity to examine the roots of the discomfort and to explore the definition of the boundaries one must keep or forego between one's personal, collegial, and professional selves.

## INSIDE OUT

As educators, then, we constantly move back and forth from "inside" to "outside"—from our most personal self to our most professional being, from reflection to interaction, from working alone to working with others, from commitment to action. The chapters that follow explore these processes in the context of the importance of congruence between our inner and outer selves.

# 2

# Inside Reflections

## Who We Are and How We See Ourselves

W e teach in accordance with what our lived experiences have been—both personally and professionally—and with what we believe about ourselves and with how we view others.

As teachers and leaders, our reflections on our individual and personal experiences become the narrative stories of our lives. These stories help provide meaning to our existence and guide us in our future endeavors (Polkinghorne, 1988; Van Manen, 1991). The stories also help us shape and reshape our experiences as we move from the old to the new—as we learn and grow. Vygotsky (1978) described learning as an internal process that takes place through our perceptions and interpretations of the experiences we have in the real world. These experiences, when translated into a narrative story, become the fabric and backdrop for the landscape of our inner journey. As Noddings (1991) claimed, "Stories have the power to direct and change our lives" (p. 157). Our perceptions and experiences are expressed in the stories we share about our children, our teaching, and our leading. In italics throughout the book, we as authors share our own personal narratives, in order to illuminate our own exploration of teaching and leading from the inside out.

*My son is an early morning philosopher who invariably wakes pondering the realities of his own existence. One early morning years ago, when he was in the sixth grade, he leaned his head through the bathroom doorway as I was brushing my teeth and commented, "I'm not as smart as I used to be."*

*Startled, I gurgled back, "Why not?"*

*"Well," he responded. "Remember when I was little. I was a lot smarter then because I was always asking questions, and I learned a lot of things. But now I spend most of my time in school, and school isn't a place for asking questions."*

*There is certainly irony in this exchange. As I gulped my morning cup of coffee and tidied the kitchen before heading out the door myself, I remembered the barrenness of my own early years of teaching—the rows of desks, the whole class lessons, my failure to acknowledge my seventh- and eighth-grade students as people who inhabited a larger reality than my classroom. I am embarrassed to admit that I taught young adolescents for four years before I realized that these things represented issues to be considered. Then, I sent my son to a parent cooperative nursery school that simply aimed to provide the best possible environment in which a child could spend a year being three or four years old. There, as a parent helper, I began to feel more and more uncomfortable about what was happening in my own classroom. I was disturbed by the contrast between the eager and involved three- and four-year-olds I saw in the morning and the spit-back-the-right-answer twelve-year-olds I saw the same afternoon. These middle schoolers had once been inquisitive, enthusiastic preschoolers, too. What had happened to them? And when? And why? What could I do to make my classroom a better environment in which a child could spend a year being twelve or thirteen* (Carr, 1993, p. 9)?

The juxtaposition of such a parental experience with our professional world highlights a mismatch between practice and beliefs that can lead to ongoing reflections and related changes based on the many facets of the answers to the question, "What are the most effective approaches to learning and teaching young adolescent students?" Our meanings and interpretations help make sense of experiences and support our beliefs about how children learn best, what teaching strategies we use, and what style of leadership we employ.

## THE USE OF LANGUAGE AND TACIT KNOWING

Our consciousness of who we are, how we make sense of the world, and how we see ourselves in the world is constantly evolving and expanding. How we understand ourselves and perceive others is a key component of how we connect to our roles as teachers and leaders (Cochran-Smith & Lytle, 1993). Central to our connections with others is our use of language. Our discourse is molded by experiences, inherited traits, gender, ethnicity, and place of origin, as well as by professional and personal beliefs and dispositions (Gilligan, 1982; Kleinfeld & Yerian, 1995; L. Smith, Skarbek, & Hurst, 2005).

Combined, these varying factors contribute and impact how we perceive those around us, how we frame our language and present ourselves to the world, and how we form our beliefs and values regarding teaching and leading. Vygotsky (1978) determined that reflective, interactive development takes place in a social context. We learn and change, to varying degrees, based upon our social interactions, life experiences, and our willingness to step into opportunities that present them selves. As we continue to mature, we develop personal beliefs about how the world functions, and we create an internal language, "inner speech," to convey those beliefs.

To explain the use of this internal language, Polanyi (1966) introduced the idea of "semantic aspect of tacit knowing." He suggested that all meaning is a projection away from ourselves and offers the analogy of a "using a tool for the first time," as a metaphor for connecting with others at an emotional level. He stated:

> Anyone using a probe for the first time will feel its impact against his fingers and palm. But as we learn to use a probe, or to use a stick for feeling our way, our awareness of its impact on our hand is transformed into a sense of its point touching the objects we are exploring. This is how an interpretative effort transposes meaningless feelings into meaningful ones, and places these at some distance from the original feeling....This is also [the case] when we use a tool. We are attending to the meaning of its impact on our hands in terms of the effect on the things to which we are applying it. We may call this the *semantic* aspect of tacit knowing. All meaning tends to be displaced away from ourselves (pp. 11–12).

Polanyi (1969) alluded to the inside-out process of connecting who we are internally (emotions, feelings, and rational thoughts) to the outer world via using as a tool the semantics, or language, of "tacit knowledge." The more we reflect on our own thoughts, feelings, and beliefs and articulate these to our colleagues, the more our tacit knowledge is developed. This internal and external dialogue enhances the fluidity and congruence of our inner and outer worlds. Thus a major factor in knowing who we are as teachers and leaders lies in developing congruence between our inner and outer selves—using the language of tacit knowledge. Ideally, this continued internal and external dialogue guides actions and behaviors that are aligned with our thoughts, feeling, and beliefs, creating a "seamless self" whose reflections, knowledge, and behaviors are consistently congruent. In areas where our internal and external dialogue is still emergent, we often see gaps between what we know or say and what we do. For example,

*In a visit to a physical education intern in her sixth week, my observation was in the gym where about thirty-five students were assembling, "dressed out" for volleyball. The students trickled in and gathered closely around the intern who began to call roll after the bell rang. The intern called each name individually and had each student raise her hand as the name was called. The intern then carefully marked each student as present or absent on the report sheet that was collected at the end of the day. I watched amused but frustrated as this process took over five minutes and the behavior of the group deteriorated, as is apt to happen when young people are bored or waiting. In addition, a couple of students left the gym after their names were called and the intern could not see over the crowd around her to see them leave. Also one or two of the students answered twice, apparently covering for truant students, without the intern noticing.*

*After calling roll, the intern began to organize scrimmage teams, which took another eight minutes, and one of the students reported quietly to the teacher that two girls had left during roll call. The intern sent that student to find the other two. As far as I could tell, the class now had about five members missing and unsupervised. The mentor teacher, who had been called to the office for another matter, came into the gym at that point and saw that the girls were busily involved in the planned activities. She came over and seemed pleased with the intern's progress. In a few minutes, three of the missing students sauntered in casually, immediately joining the activities when they saw the mentor teacher.*

*In the debrief, with both the mentor and the intern present, I asked if the mentor teacher could start the next class, which was also a girl's volleyball class. The mentor teacher did so by organizing the scrimmage teams as the girls appeared from the locker room so that the activities were in full swing by the time the bell rang. She then took roll by looking around the gym for each girl because she knew each one by name. In the second debrief, the intern was asked to describe the beginning of class processes used by the mentor teacher. I then asked about the missing students. The mentor teacher saw immediately the potential problem of students truant and unsupervised and of sending another student, with no hall pass, to retrieve them. The intern protested that she couldn't see students leaving and didn't know the students' names well enough to handle roll call as the mentor had done. Ultimately, the intern recognized the importance of getting class started quickly, and until she could learn students' names, she walked around the gym calling out the names as the girls continued their activities. The mentor teacher noted that she had not explicitly taught the intern these processes. Her own well-developed tacit knowledge had blinded her to the need for such elemental instructions.*

The tacit knowledge of the mentor teacher gave her the tools to streamline the beginning of class routine. The intern, whose tacit knowledge was underdeveloped at this point, did not have the tools or skills to begin the class efficiently. Nor did she have tools for on-the-spot decision making that protected the safety of the truant girls and her own efficacy as the teacher responsible for all students. Although the intern could recognize and articulate the importance of these instruction and safety issues, she could not yet act upon them seamlessly and effortlessly—an aspect of "with-it-ness" that comes only with experience.

Teachers and leaders spend years learning to be more effective: developing particular skills such as "with-it-ness," exploring various classroom management tools, learning specific leadership techniques to help facilitate truly professional learning communities (PLCs), and discovering effective ways to engage students' minds. As human beings, we spend a lifetime understanding the complexities of who we are. We explore our motives, clarify our intentions, and learn how to interface our inner world of thoughts, feelings, and beliefs with the outer world of people (students, teachers, administrators, etc.), things (institutions, political structures, family, etc.), and actions (teaching, leading, doing, etc.). Even with all of the varied experiences, learning, and change in our lives, we may still not be able to "see" and articulate certain aspects of our professional development. If we have relied predominantly on our strengths, then we may be blinded to aspects of our weaknesses. For instance, if we favor the inner world of thoughts, feelings, and ideas, we may have blind spots about the outer world of people and actions. The following narrative illuminates the difficulty of "not seeing" that we sometimes face in our teaching:

> *After four years of learning how to be a teacher, and with an earnest heart set on teaching kindergarten, I was quickly disheartened to learn that jobs in the early 1980s in my region were few and far apart. After months of substitute teaching in a wide range of school settings, I was approached by Randy Brown, the principal, to teach seven multihandicapped children with profound developmental delays in a segregated school for students with challenges.*
>
> *The children were bussed in daily from a twenty-four-hour housing facility, as parents of these children often sent them there to be raised by the state. I had had no training and, in truth, knew nothing about the needs of these children whose individual education plan included literally breathing skills, learning to walk, controlling seizures, and doing physical therapy on limbs that became so rigid that it took two people to loosen them up. One particular sixteen-year-old girl, whom I*

*will call Jennifer, often unnerved me. Her seizures were frequent and very intense—lasting minutes. Her body would either be so limber that she was unable to sit or become so rigid and stiff that very little could be done to help her.*

*I was afraid of failing in this job and of the repercussions that it might have on future teaching positions. From this, I began to develop a false positive mask. As a first year teacher, teaching out of field, wanting to become full-time, I would wear a smile to work and pretend to be happy. In essence, I masked my true feelings. I was genuinely optimistic about being hired, learning the ropes of teaching—communication, community building, and being a caring educator. However, underneath this was a deep fear of these children's anomalies and physical realities and of my own inadequacy to teach them.*

*One day after returning from lunch, I noticed a woman standing looking down at Jennifer, whose body was taut and quivering on the mat. The woman was crying quietly to herself. It was Jennifer's mother, who had stopped by to visit her daughter. She would not touch her daughter—the third triplet to be born. Instead, she left to pick up her "gifted child" from the school next door—the first born of the three. In the moment of her mother's leaving, Jennifer became real and whole to me, and I began to lose my mask and start my journey as an authentic teacher of all children.*

This story illustrates the difficulty of maintaining congruence with the inner self while representing a partial or false outer self to others. Simply being vulnerable and saying to other colleagues or to the principal, "I'm scared and I don't know how to make sense of this," seemed impossible at the time. Instead, pretense took over—"I can do this, and not only do it, but do it with a smile and no one needs to know that I'm struggling and don't know how to handle the children's behaviors." The ability to speak one's truth matures with experience, ongoing reflection, and the development of emotional maturity (Goleman, Boyatzis, & McKee, 2002) and emotional intelligence (Goleman, 1995) over time.

## THE DEVELOPMENT OF EMOTIONAL INTELLIGENCE

Goleman (1995) outlined five primary elements of emotional intelligence: self-awareness, self-mastery or self-management of emotions, motivation, empathy or social awareness, and relationship management. Each is interconnected and, to some extent, can be learned. However, being self-aware is the fundamental ability of emotional intelligence (EI). Specific dimensions of EI have been found to be reliable predictors for successful educators. Stone, James, Parker, and Wood (2005) suggested,

> professional development programs would be wise to focus on promoting or developing the following abilities:

> - emotional self-awareness (the ability to recognize and understand one's feelings and emotions);
> - self-actualization (the ability to tap potential capacities and skills in order to improve oneself);
> - empathy (the ability to be attentive to, understand, and appreciate the feelings of others);
> - interpersonal relationships (the ability to establish and maintain mutually satisfying relationships);
> - flexibility (the ability to adjust one's emotions, thoughts, and behaviors to changing situations and conditions);
> - problem solving (the ability to identify and define problems as well as to generate potentially effective solutions); [and]
> - impulse control (the ability to resist or delay emotional behaviors) (p. 34).

These skills are critical in the relationships between ourselves and other professionals. Development of these skills is indicative of the corresponding development of tacit knowledge that can be our tool for harmonizing our inner and outer selves.

The study of emotional intelligence is but one example of a growing focus in education on assessing personal characteristics and abilities. In the past several decades, there has been

a consistent interest in research focusing on personality characteristics, or traits, in relationship to teacher effectiveness
(Reid, 1999; Rushton, Knopp, & R. L. Smith, 2006; Sears,
Kennedy, Kaye, & Gail, 1997). Using different personality
inventories, educators and researchers have studied whether
or not certain dispositions—for instance, "caring"—can pre-
dispose one to be a more effective teacher (L. Smith et al.,
2005). Marso and Pigge's (1990) work aimed at uncovering
patterns of traits explored teachers grouped by grade level,
major field, and size of community. These studies showed, for
example, that student interns at the junior high level tended to
be "extraverted, well-adjusted, warm, friendly, and participating," while those student teachers at the senior high school
level were "intelligent, enthusiastic, and practical." They also
found that effective teachers in small towns tend to be
reserved, shy, sensitive, trusting, and introverted. Thus certain
cultural variables associated with size of community are
strong determinants of the particular patterns of teachers' personality traits that are related to classroom effectiveness
(Marso & Pigge, 1990).

Knowing one's temperament and personality is important
for teachers so they can recognize the differences between their
personality types and their students' learning styles (A. M.
Fairhurst & L. L. Fairhurst, 1995). Similarly, school leaders'
awareness of their own personality types can facilitate interaction and communication with teachers, even more readily
when the teachers' types are also known. Imagine the natural
strengths of a sixth-grade teacher being related to such
attributes as "favors detailed planning," "is concise in her presentation of material," "enjoys making decisions," "dislikes
ambiguity," "is well organized," and "is sequentially logical."
Now, imagine if this teacher has a student in class whose natural abilities focus on broader areas such as exploring creative
ideas, using a vivid imagination to plot strategies in his mind,
and easily seeing differences among ideas being presented. If
the teacher's focus is on her strengths and assumes that her
student's abilities are similar, a problem may arise between the

two. Indeed, the student may be viewed as a "nonconformist" or a "trouble maker," while the student may perceive the teacher as "boring," "dull," and "strict."

Jung (1969) developed and expanded a theory of human personality based on typologies of human behavior that was later used to create the Myers-Briggs Type Indicator—a tool to discover our strengths. Jung believed that the human psyche has an ability to heal itself as it seeks for balance. He proposed that as we mature, our free choice allows us to embrace the positive experiences we have and to adapt and integrate those negative life experiences into a more whole self. He centered his attention on the *potential* gifts that people naturally inherit and live by (A. M. Fairhurst & L. L. Fairhurst, 1995). However, he also believed that our "one-sidedness" could lead to mal-adaptive behaviors if we did not pay attention to it.

All of these assessments and studies of personal skills and behaviors point to a compelling factor that informs our inner and outer development: The differences among people that first can cause us not to recognize or understand the work or behavior of others and that second can blind us to aspects of ourselves that prevent us from relating to others as effectively as possible. In other words, by the very nature of our skills and personalities—because we have relative strengths and weaknesses in both—we invariably have blind spots that can both get in the way of our work and relationships and prevent us from seeing our own strengths and gifts.

## ACKNOWLEDGING OUR BLIND SPOTS TO IMPROVE THE WORK WE DO

Our blind spots are those aspects of our thinking and behavior that we do not always perceive. They are hidden from our view and our consciousness but may indeed have an influence on how we teach and lead. They are often a part of our under-developed natures that resides in the unconscious and which others see first, particularly in times of stress (Jung, 1969). It is a bit like standing before a mirror, where we see ourselves and believe that what we are viewing is the image of who we are and how others see us. We believe we look a particular way, and each time we view ourselves in the mirror, we reinforce that image and belief about ourselves. Due to the reversal of any mirror image, however, our left side is actually on our right and vice versa. In truth, we only see the reverse image of what others see when they look at us, and throughout our lives, we never see ourselves exactly as others see us. One variation on this idea is the "imposter syndrome" (Clance & Imes, 1978; Harvey & Katz, 1985) in which people who have achieved success are fearful that they are not efficacious or talented and that, by being open and authentic, they expose themselves as "imposters," not really capable at all. Our self-doubt and potential lack of congruity between the mirror images of ourselves can impede and delimit our professional work. Until we have others mirror for us our capabilities as well as our blind spots and until we are willing to accept the fear of being exposed, the underdeveloped areas continue to encumber our teaching and leading. Being less mature and well developed than our favored areas, our underdeveloped areas may come out sideways in unsettling ways (Jung, 1969; Quenk, 1993).

> Early in my teaching career, I worked at a school where there were strong disagreements among some of the teachers in my department. One colleague in particular had a tendency to overpower me when I disagreed with her. She would begin to talk nonstop, to belittle my work, and to question my competence. Each time this happened, I would cry. At first, I was as taken aback by my own response as I was by my colleague's unprofessional behavior. Soon, I realized I was reacting from a place of discomfort with conflict left over from my childhood. I began to read about conflict and about how to cope with difficult people (Bramson, 1988), and soon I had new strategies to try when confronted by my colleague. If I called her name, she would pause, and I had an opportunity to insert what was important that I say. I no longer cried in my professional work, and as I changed,

*my colleague changed how she dealt with me. Never did we become friends, but we became colleagues who could disagree professionally and respectfully. "Seeing" my blind side, the underdeveloped aspects of my professional self, helped me to build congruence between my inner and outer selves.*

Quenk (1993) used the term *shadow* to personify those areas in our personalities that we do not readily see. She suggested that the shadow, our blind side, is a "major component of a person's personal unconscious, a layer of the psyche that is more accessible than its much larger counterpart, the collective unconscious" (p. 51). Acknowledging and exploring the shadows may help us to engage in a higher quality of teaching and leading.

Blind spots can impede our work as teachers. Through review of teacher practices in mathematics and analysis of mathematics textbooks designed by mathematics experts, Nathan, Alibali, and Koedinger (2001) defined the concept of expert blind spot as follows:

> The inability to perceive the difficulties that novices will experience as they approach a new domain of knowledge. In education it is manifest as the tendency for content area experts to perceive the organization of the domain of study as the central structure for organizing students' learning experiences, rather than basing instruction on students actual developmental processes. (p. 3)

At times, the content knowledge of the expert teacher impedes application of pedagogical content knowledge about how students would best learn mathematics. The expert teachers are blinded, essentially, by their expertise and inability to place themselves in the "shoes" of the novice learner.

*I was teaching secondary methods courses in a weekend degree program at a small college when a student brought to me the opportunity to have available on campus a "Project Wild" workshop offered through the state Fish and Wildlife*

*Department. The "Project Wild" curriculum incorporated numerous hands-on activities responsive to various of the intelligences identified by Gardener's (1983) multiple intelligences theory. The workshop was well attended by my students, who viewed me as a "hard but fair, heavy on the reading and writing assignments" sort of professor. I participated right alongside them, and I was thoroughly enjoying myself, until the "make your own fish" activity was introduced. Each of us was given a package of sticks of hard clay in various colors and told to use the clay to create one of the types of fish we had learned about in the previous exercise. I am very unskilled when it comes to anything "arts and crafty," and I felt a sense of panic begin to rise inside me. Hard as I tried, I couldn't get the clay to look much like a fish of any kind. Yet my students, especially, the students who struggled with writing assignments in my classes, it seemed, were producing masterpieces!*

Just as students tend to favor one set of skills or learning styles over another, teachers and leaders also have preferences. As educators, we tend to favor one particular side or aspect of our personalities in both our teaching and leadership styles (A. M. Fairhurst & L. L. Fairhurst, 1995). We focus upon and develop qualities that are natural for us and often avoid those areas that make us feel uncomfortable. It is important to recognize that these "underdeveloped" areas, once developed and brought into consciousness, could possibly be of equal or greater benefit to our teaching (Quenk, 1993).

## FOCUS FOR REFLECTION, EXPLORATION, AND ACTION: EXPLORING WHO WE TRULY ARE

Our thoughts, feelings, beliefs, and tacit knowledge as well as our blind spots define our teaching and enter the classroom as our "shadow" (Quenk, 1993; see also L. Smith et al., 2005). Motivations, intentions, and actions as well as the blind side and unconscious factors are important to explore and develop, particularly if there is to be congruence between our inner and outer selves.

Try surfacing your blind spots by illuminating the differences between what you view as important to you and how this compares to your actual allocations of time.

- Divide a sheet of paper in half and draw two equal size circles, one above the other.
- In the top circle, pinpoint the center and draw radius lines from the center to the outer ridge creating separate and different pieces of the circle.
- Each piece of the pie represents a part of your life that is important to you (family, job, gender, teacher, traveling, etc.). The degree of importance is determined by the size of the pie. This first pie represents the degree of importance this area has for you, not the amount of time spent with these different facets.
- On the second circle beneath, do the same exercise. This time, allow each piece of the pie to represent the amount of time that you actually engage in this area during your day, week, or month.

What do you notice? Are you aligned with what you say is important to you, or like most of us, is there a discrepancy between what you say is important and the amount of time you actually are engaged with those activities? What are the implications for your work as a teacher or as a leader in your school or district? Do the areas to which you devote less time represent underdeveloped skills, behaviors, or even potential blind spots? Could further exploration and development in any of these underdeveloped skills or behaviors facilitate the alignment of your time with what you deem most important in your professional work?

Another way to reflect on who we are and how we see is to use a "third thing" (Palmer, 2004) as a stimulus to bring to the surface a perception, experience, or need that has long been hidden from view. A "third thing" can be a poem, a saying, a picture, or a word on which one chooses to reflect and then respond. For example, try holding in mind an area of your work where there is currently some tension. Use a picture, poem, or saying as a vehicle through which to describe what is happening currently with that area of work. What does the picture, poem, or saying suggest to you about yourself and your work? What do you wonder? What do you enjoy? What do you wish to change? What do you need?

Also consider inviting a close colleague or friend to engage in this process with you—someone who listens carefully without giving advice or trying to fix the problem. This can bring new awareness to our sense of our selves and our work. To be listened to by someone who does no more than ask "open, honest questions" (Palmer, 2004)—questions for which there is no outside agenda—is to have the experience of a witness who simply holds us in the safe place as we make connections back to ourselves, back to the essential essence that brought us to teaching and leading in the first place, and back to seeing ourselves as we truly are.

# 3

# Outside Manifestations

## Nurturing Authenticity and Integrity

Often as teachers and leaders we "fly" through the week, grading papers, teaching, attending staff meetings, speaking with parents, and budgeting our precious time to make each minute count.

In this hurried space, our emphasis is often on others—the child, the parent, and colleagues. Indeed, our pace influences perceptions, emotions, and behaviors. Acknowledging the fast pace of our lives and its effects on us is an important first step in creating time and space for reflection and authentic engagement—for honoring ourselves. Without making time for reflection and engagement, we have little chance of developing or maintaining the deliberate authenticity and integrity of effective teachers and leaders.

"Authentic teachers and leaders are aware of how the context of teaching influences them and their teaching relationships" (Carusetta & Cranton, 2005, p. 294). With each interaction, we make various choices and decisions that impact students, fellow teachers, and ourselves. Many of these decisions appear inconsequential, yet each choice, like each brushstroke on a canvas, eventually becomes the portrait of our lives. *Authentic* is used here to describe true and honest congruence between self and action. Authentic teaching requires the educator to create a framework for acknowledging one's self and for reflecting inwardly as to the very nature of who and what we are. To nurture authenticity and integrity is to know the truth of one's realities and relationships, to honor one's convictions, and to act on one's sense of purpose and commitment.

Authenticity comes through having a critical knowledge of the context in which we work and seeing the principal contradictions of that society. To be authentic, the educator is bold, dares to take risks, and recognizes that he or she will not always win over people (Friere, 1972, as cited in Carusetta & Cranston, 2005, p. 294).

In exploring authenticity and integrity, considering several factors can help clarify the ways in which teachers and leaders demonstrate these characteristics. First, the impact of emotions on professional work and behavior is explored, specifically risk taking, openness, and integrity. Second, the process of trust building and consequent emergence of trusting relationships is examined. Next, we explore multiplicity of roles for teachers and leaders in a context of ambiguity and the finding of our "voice." Finally, the importance of reflection is discussed and demonstrated.

## EMOTIONS AND AUTHENTICITY

"Understanding the powerful role of emotions in the workplace sets the best leaders apart from the rest" (Goleman, Boyatzis, & McKee, 2002, p. 4). Exceptional teachers and leaders tend to be more open about their feelings, beliefs, and behaviors, which in turn creates a level of perceived authenticity, a palpable yet unseen presence. "Such leaders openly admit their mistakes or faults, and confront unethical behavior in others rather than turn a blind eye" (Goleman et al., 2002, p. 254). These leaders invite scrutiny and feedback while transcending personally limiting barriers such as fear or self-consciousness. Possibly the greatest risk we take as teachers and leaders is to actually transcend these boundaries established to protect ourselves and to create "interpersonal safety zone" (Kouzes & Posner, 1999). "If we don't open and express our affection and appreciation, then we stay safe behind the wall of rationality" (p. 12). We can easily focus on appearances of success or avoidance of conflict and potential failure. Opportunities for communication and growth, both individual and collective, can be lost. Reflection, genuine engagement, and opening and exposing the self to those we teach and lead help dissolve boundaries of interpersonal safety, as illustrated in the following story.

*Once while visiting school, I watched the principal interact with some of his students. The principal was sitting at a small table outside of the classroom speaking with individual students. I immediately noticed the relaxed presence of both the student and the principal. It was one of respect and mutual appreciation as he "chatted" with children of all abilities and developmental levels. He talked to the students as though they were adults, sharing with them what he was doing during the day, what he ate for lunch, that his dog dug up the neighbors flowers, as well as finding out how the children were behaving in class and what they were studying. At the end of the conversation, he encouraged the student to have a mindful day and gave the child a smiley face on his paper. I asked the principal about his interactions, and he said that he made it a point to know every student in his school by name and on a one to one basis. His belief was that opening himself up to the students through contact and ordinary conversation helped to create a mutual respect between him and the students who attended his school.*

Self-awareness and being outwardly open are two essential aspects of being authentic. Looking at this principal from the outside, such characteristics seem logical and doable. When looking from the inside at the prospect of enacting these qualities ourselves, fears can emerge: "How could I possibly do that? What will they think?" J. Tompkins (1990) articulated with vivid truth these elements of authenticity in her paper, *Pedagogy of the Distressed.* She stated that her need to teach was born not from a heart to teach students to learn, but rather, from a desire to show them how knowledgeable and smart she was and how prepared for class she was in an effort more focused on having them think well of her than on helping them to learn. Until she was able to move beyond these self-absorbed motivations, she could not authentically engage her students.

Similarly, we can deceive ourselves through unfounded justifications for our decisions as teachers and leaders. The Arbinger Institute (2002) described one's choice not to do what one feels is right as a form of self-betrayal. For example, in your grade-level team meeting, a new teacher shares that she is struggling with student discipline. You see that she needs support and assistance, but because you are planning a hiking trip for the weekend and must go for groceries that evening, you decline to stay after the meeting to help her. Thus you have chosen not to "honor" your feeling and, in a sense, have betrayed yourself by ignoring what you think is best. A myriad of justifications creeps into your thoughts. "The teacher should have learned this already. I am over-worked anyway and resent spending extra time at school." Soon resentment and negativity surround the decision. The Arbinger Institute referred to this as "being in the box" (p. 79) and as seeking justification for what we did or did not choose to do. In justifying our actions, we inflate our own abilities and virtues while inflating others' shortcomings.

Ultimately, we can consistently deceive ourselves by not honoring our genuine feelings in the first place. Our decisions and motivations are no longer congruent with our actions, and we become inauthentic. Only through careful reflection and intentional thoughtfulness can we maintain the desired congruity. In sum, with honesty and nurturing of self, congruence develops within us and authenticity becomes a way of being, teaching, and leading.

## TRUSTING THE PROCESS

Congruity between the inner and outer selves creates trust in others. Trust, defined as a predictable repetition of behaviors and outcomes (Galvin & Fauske, 2000; Ring, 2003), allows people to predict responses from others and to know what to expect in a situation. It provides a degree of comfort that emerges over time and continued association with others in an increasingly familiar environment. Predicting others' responses accurately can allow risk taking when the culture encourages and supports it. Trust also provides space for authenticity in interactions among group members in a collegial environment where competing positions, goals, and ideas for solutions are processed systematically and openly over time, allowing for full disclosure, examination, and exploration. Collegiality does not require full agreement among all group members. Rather, differences are respected and treated seriously and respectfully in discussions. Personal positions of advocacy and agendas for change are made transparent. We do not avoid conflict, but rather we embrace dialogue and mutual adaptation. Authentic collegiality is realized through transparent and sincere participation by all parties. Transparency of motive is key; it removes suspicion and mistrust to declare one's position and to be open about the outcome that one hopes for. Transparency must in turn be accompanied by willingness to accept alternative views and solutions that can create a winning outcome for all parties rather than just for one's own agenda. This combination of transparency of motive and openness to alternative views are the backbones of authentic integrity in teachers and leaders.

Achieving this level of authenticity prescribes that we attend to intentionality in developing collegial cultures. Intentionality implies knowledge of characteristics of professional community, expertise in implementing appropriate processes and structures, and the capacity to let these structures guide people to consistent interactive dialogue and action with integrity. Manipulation, on the other hand, can occur when we have knowledge and expertise but are unable or unwilling to step back from the participatory process, to trust the process. Trusting the process ourselves and allowing the development of mutually trustful relationships over time are imperative to authentic teaching and leadership.

Consider a comparative study of three middle schools where teaming was implemented by middle school principals who had knowledge of good practice for building trust and professional community through middle school teams (Schelble & Fauske, 2000). Teaming structures, content, and focus differed according to principal leadership approach and "style." These principals also differed in their level of control over or intervention in the teaming process. In other words, they differed in willingness to trust the process.

School A was implementing grade-level teams for the first time during the school year studied. The principal supported the concept of middle-level school structures and programs and was in the second year as principal at the school with experience with middle school reform. School A had eight teams of three to four teachers representing the subject areas of English, science, and social studies for each grade. Counselors, electives, and special needs teachers were not team members. Team leaders were selected by the principal, and team minutes were not required. Principal A believed that change is an evolutionary process whereby teaming would develop over time and focused more on the natural development of teams. Hence, this principal is described as a "developer." This belief clearly impacted the work of the teams. Although the principal's stated outcome of having teachers being "caring, academically effective and communicating with each other" was also articulated in teacher interviews, in the actual work of the teams, teachers remained unclear as to why they were teaming. Leadership direction was focused on presenting information and allowing teachers time to assimilate that information rather than on directing teacher teams through their work. Emphasis was on professional development activities that provided the teams with opportunities to be exposed to the concept of teaming (giving them opportunities to rub shoulders with others who are teaming, inviting other schools who team to "tell their stories" to the faculty). A consultant was also used for professional development. Teaming became the vehicle for introducing teachers to the belief that teacher teams should support students in developing feelings of belong and becoming secure, confident, and successful.

School B had been involved in middle school reform for five years. The principal had been at the school for six years and acted as an advocate of the middle school philosophy, having secured several grants to support reform efforts including teacher teaming. The three teams were structured as grade-level teams of twelve to fifteen teachers representing all subjects including special needs. Team leaders were elected by the team. Teams met every Friday afternoon from one until three o'clock and turned in minutes to the principal after each meeting. The principal took a systemic approach toward creating a common vision and encouraging collaboration, and the school focused on providing the preset programs for collaboration (e.g., Community of Caring).

The influence of the School B principals' style of creating collaborative structures and facilitating site-based decision making impacted the decision making and management of the school. This principal had a take-charge approach and played a central decision-making role in directing the teams' work. Thus teaming became the "vehicle" by which the school conducted many aspects of its business. Through the teaming structure, for example, the school applied for grants (i.e., state-level funds for "excellent" schools), made grade-level decisions, and selected professional development activities. Because this principal "created" the teaming structure and roles at the school, the term *creator* was used to describe this principal's approach.

Although School C had been involved in limited levels of teaming in past years, this was the first year of full implementation of grade-level teams and the principal's first year at the school. The principal had implemented teaming at a previous junior high school in the district. The principal was a strong advocate of the middle school philosophy, had extensive experience in implementing teaming, and had knowledge of its benefits to teachers and students. The teams were structured as three grade-level teams of twelve to fifteen teachers representing all subjects including special needs. Team leaders were elected by the team. Teams met every Wednesday afternoon from one until three o'clock and turned in progress reports on their goals and projects to the principal after each meeting. This principal's belief that schools should be learning communities for teachers as well as students provided the direction of team development. Professional development activities were structured around creating a culture where collaboration and teaming became the norm (i.e., acknowledging the need to develop a common definition of teaming for the school, building relationships and trust before introducing content, and focusing on implementing what the literature says about middle-level student needs). This principal shared professional articles and research and systematically collected information from the staff about their needs for staff development. The principal then presented a summary of the feedback back to the staff and built the professional development plan based on their input integrated with information gathered from journal articles and consultants. The teachers were expected and encouraged to "make sense of teaming" by reflecting on best practice as described in studies and by consultants and their own experience. The principal's intended outcome was to create a culture where teachers worked together to address the academic, social, and emotional needs of middle-level students. Teaming was only one means of achieving that goal.

The comparison and analysis of these three scenarios sheds light on the ways in which principals can establish processes for authentic engagement. In the first scenario, the principal gives too little direction and creates confusion over the task as well as how to participate effectively. The teachers in that school ultimately went to the principal with suggestions for alternate ways of organizing themselves for teaming, and the principal took the plan to the faculty where it was consequently adopted and implemented. The principal in this school, while somewhat clumsy in his initial steps, was participating genuinely, was open to new ideas, and was respectful of teachers' expertise. Teaming in this school thrived over time.

In the second scenario, the principal implemented teaming quite efficiently, garnering resources from the district and being fairly clear about structure, tasks, and decision-making processes. Teachers in the school diligently turned in minutes from the team meetings and rarely missed a team meeting because the team leader had to take roll and prepare minutes. The principal, however, sent mixed messages about the importance of teaming and about the authority of the team to make decisions. Both the principal and the assistant principal frequently interrupted team meetings for announcements that usually were made over the intercom after school, but that were supposed to be eliminated on team meeting days for the stated reason of not interrupting. Also the principal over-turned decisions of the teams. In one case, the seventh-grade team wanted to offer more "honors" sections of English, and the principal refused to do so with no explanation to the team. Consequently, the teams were kept off balance (in disequilibrium) about the parameters of their authority. Teaming in this school continued, or rather, the team meetings and minute taking continued, but the teachers used the time surreptitiously to address instructional and student concerns of their own agenda. Interestingly, the minutes included only a basic description of the parts of the meeting pertaining to the principal's directives. The bulk of time was spent on other matters important to the teachers. Although teaming was successful in meeting some of the teachers' needs, team members were not authentically engaged in the teaming process as conceived by the principal. Likewise, the principal in this school was not fully genuine and authentic in implementation of teaming with genuine tasks and commensurate authority.

The principal in scenario three implemented teams in a process that grew from dialogue and information gathering in which teachers played a substantial role. The principal advocated a certain strategy, adjusted that strategy according to teacher feedback, and then watched the process unfold under the teachers' own auspices. Teachers identified and completed meaningful tasks and were clear about the parameters of their authority. They turned in projects that informed teaching and learning instead of minutes that only partially reflected the work of the teams. The teachers in School C had greater ownership of teaming and used the process to enhance both their work and their relationships. Principal C was described as a "builder" of professional relationships and trust.

We know a good deal about processes building relationships and trust; yet when teachers and leaders have implemented these processes to invite dialogue, shared decision-making, and collaborative problem solving, they often intervene in or disengage from the process. We are not authentically engaged when we intervene out of fear and discomfort, sometimes because the group has drifted away from the parameters of their task or sometimes when the group is deadlocked. Teacher and leaders also can disengage because of their own feelings of inadequacy, a misguided notion that delegation means hands off, or the lack of a deep commitment to the effort. These three scenarios illustrate that in order for teachers and leaders to be genuine and authentic collaborators, they must trust the process. Even when we make mistakes, we can be viewed as authentically engaged when we participate in the process openly. For example, a school leader may introduce a plan for schoolwide collaborative project but cannot know the outcomes of the collaborative process without letting the process unfold. The school leader is dependent on the participants in the project plan for their interpretation and commitment to the purposes. The road may be bumpy and the plan may undergo multiple revisions. There may be unexpected outcomes, both positive and negative. Nevertheless, the school moves ahead, learning together over time as the plan unfolds, taking risks on new ideas, and developing trusting relationships and mutual openness. Mutually authentic participation based on genuinely shared authority, respect, and values are the constitution of teaching and leading from the inside out.

## INTUITION AND "VOICE"

The process of building trusting relationships requires that we intentionally create time and space for honoring and reflecting on our inner, authentic feelings. "Any authentic call ultimately comes from the voice of the teacher within, the voice that invites me to honor the nature of my true self" (Palmer, 1998, p. 29). Just as mothers nurture the needs of their children, many of us become teachers to impart knowledge and help our students learn and grow. Likewise, leaders in our schools often serve their teachers selflessly. Nurturing of self requires listening to one's intuitive voice and acknowledging the needs that exist within us. Palmer (2000) observed that the "soul speaks its truth only under quiet, inviting, and trustworthy conditions" (p. 7). Sometimes it takes the ordinary events to capture our attention and wake us up to opportunities because we ignore those quiet reminders in our bustling days. Our inner, intuitive voice is drowned out by extraneous background noise.

Our intuitive side is expressed through our connection with others. Intuition, that essential leadership ability to apply not just technical expertise but also life wisdom in making business decisions, comes naturally to the self-aware leader. Why should an intuitive sense have any place in business today, amid the plethora of hard data available to leaders? Because attuning to our feelings, according to neurological research, helps us to find the meaning in data, and so leads to better decision. Our emotional memory banks thus enable us to judge information efficiently. Emotions, science tells us, are part of the rationality, not opposed to it (Goleman et al., 2002, p. 42).

Once we have slowed down the pace of the day and are listening to our inner voice speak, we can notice more readily that which is transpiring around us. Noticing how we are "being" in relation to ourselves, to our colleagues and to the profession at large helps us to begin aligning our inner and outer selves.

## INTEGRITY—PUTTING IT ALL TOGETHER

"Good teaching cannot be reduced to technique; good teaching comes from the identity and integrity of the teacher" (Palmer, 1998, p. 10). Integrity, in and of itself, is not a final destination. It is a process of living, redefining, adjusting, and course correcting. Integrity is our innate and inherent ability to know who we are and how we truly want to live, personally and professionally. In truth, no doubt many of us would change some of the choices we have made. Being honest with ourselves is a key to developing our sense of authenticity, which inevitably leads to a life of integrity. "Integrity includes going beyond honesty. Honesty is telling the truth, and conforming reality to our words—in other words, keeping promises and fulfilling expectations. This requires an integrated character, a oneness, primarily with self but also with life" (Covey, 1992, pp. 195–196). Aligning to our actions and behavior our words and our stated intentions is living a life of integrity.

There are two parts to living a life of integrity: knowing who we are and doing what we say. Yet it is sometimes difficult to achieve congruity between these two elements when we have not articulated our true beliefs and motivations, and we encounter one of our blind spots. The important discovery of knowing the self and understanding what motivates us in our outwardly expressions is critical in understanding how and why we sometimes do not do as we say. Integrity, at one level, is saying what you mean and acting accordingly in a manner that is congruent with authentic self-knowledge. It has to do with an intrinsic state of honesty and with being content and secure with one's self.

Where does intrinsic security come from? It doesn't come from what other people think of us or how they treat us. It doesn't come from the scripts they've handed us. It doesn't come from our circumstances or our positions. It comes from within. It comes from accurate paradigms and correct principles deep in our own mind and heart. It comes from inside-out congruence, from living a life of integrity in which our daily habits reflect our deepest values (Covey, 1992, p. 298).

What motivates teachers and principals to take on these roles? Are we motivated out of a state or a need to succeed, to be recognized, or even to be loved? None of these is unacceptable, yet dressing the motivation up as something different may cloud reality and send mixed signals that dilute the intention, lessening our perceived integrity and diminishing the intrinsic security that comes from living life with congruity from the inside out.

Herein lies in the gray area between inside and outside, a boundary crossing space in which we often find ourselves.

Consider participation in team decision making as a teacher or leader. It is a space where we face artificial dichotomies. Am I an equal member of this group or do I have little to offer or say? Am I a part of this team, or am I leading the team? How can I lead and participate simultaneously? It is a space created by either/or mentalities. Is something fact or fiction, good or bad, cold or hot, or inside or outside?

By reframing these questions, we can create a space where either/or dichotomies and forced choices are not helpful or necessary, a space that has been described as living in the slash (Fine, 1994). In this space, we are not required to look at the processes as good or bad, or from the inside or outside, but we can glide through the boundaries exploring ourselves as authentic and collegial persons and professionals who are agents and appreciators of growth and change. We continually, almost relentlessly, glide among our various selves in reading this book and in our lives, never fully in one dimension but always straddling the lines. Atkinson (2001) aptly described this process as presenting her "multiple, messy selves in a way that relates to the selves of other[s], while inviting new insights by making strange those aspects of identity which otherwise seem so familiar" (p. 308). She offered a reconceptualization that captures the notions of blurred boundaries and ambiguous spaces—not as *either/or* but as *and*: mother *and* worker, tutor *and* student, rule maker *and* rule breaker (p. 311). As applied here, we can consider the multiple roles that educators play and the juxtaposition of our multiple roles, inside and outside our selves.

Each of us simultaneously fulfills a multitude of roles and expectations that blend across personal, collegial, and professional dimensions of our selves. We do not have to choose between being a member of the group and being a leader to the group. We are both. As we explore the dimensions of our selves, we can begin to be comfortable in the gray space that is our messy selves in action. We recognize an individual continuum of "inside outness" rather than being bounded by a falsely imposed dichotomy.

## Focus for Reflection, Exploration, and Action: Reflective Journaling

The process of reflective journaling, both structured and unstructured, has gained much popularity in recent years as a means of greater self-awareness and a better understanding of our intentions and behaviors in our lives and in our work (Sommer, 1989). Journaling provides a means of self-expression by helping us clarify our natural inner voice. Grennan (1989) suggested that journaling helps us to express what needs to be shared in a safe context, without having to pay attention to a particular form, audience, or evaluation. Reflective journaling can be an important process by which we can discover more about who we are as teachers and leaders. As teachers and leaders, we can make meaning and understand our own inner landscapes by taking the time to reflect and journal (Killion, 1999).

As a professional development tool, journaling can help teachers to record their perceptions of the classroom and discover more about their own teaching practices. It can help develop congruity between what we espouse to do and what we actually do in practice. Believing that the process of writing solidifies thoughts, Killion (1999) stated, "When a learner is required to apply language to an idea, the idea takes shape and form" (p. 36). Further, "Writing can be a kind of learning in itself, a way to get more control over our lives and experiences, grapple with our thoughts, and grow as humans" (Tchudi & Mitchell, as cited in Glenn, 2004, p. 35). The creative process of reflective writing can draw us to a deeper level of self-awareness as well as help unfold the complexities of our professional lives.

Taking time to write our thoughts and reflections allows for the real experiences of life to be recorded in concrete terms, in essence freezing time and thereby allowing our visible thoughts to be critically examined (Glenn, 2004). Through our writings, we see the tangible evidence of our mental processes in print, and this allows us to interact with, expand upon, and create more transformative views through examining our writing as representative of our selves. Reflective journaling can help teachers and leaders better understand their motives, practices, and teaching skills and can lead to making real changes (Glenn, 2004; Wellington & Austin, 1996). In addition, sharing our discoveries with others through a reflective journaling process can lead to greater openness and trust.

Various types of journaling can help us to examine our work as teachers and leaders.

1. **Reflection journal.** Keeping a writing journal close by to record some of those moments in which we interact with a child, a parent, or another teacher is one way to help us record important moments for later reflection and capture opportunities for authentic engagement and reflection. Reflection is aided by regularity of response, for example, writing in the journal every day or every other day. If there seems nothing to write about, simply begin to write. What comes into focus as you write? What recent happenings merit exploration? What do you wonder?

2. **Representation journal.** Sometimes it useful to collect pictures, poems, and other artifacts to represent in mostly wordless ways our responses to our world and our work. Making a regular practice of clipping pictures from magazines and newspapers, finding "favorite sayings" in books or on the Internet, writing out poems that capture our attention, and/or drawing or including cards and other artwork over time can create a very different form of representation of what is important to us in our lives at home and at work. A colleague collecting these sorts of artifacts created a 365-day journal with a saying or drawing on each page. Then, throughout the year, she used the "artifact of the day" as a stimulus to reflect upon and write about her work.

3. **Structured journal.** Here is a simple example of keeping a structured journal that can help focus attention

on the moment. It involves four steps completed in four columns:

- **Step 1.** In the first column, enter the date.
- **Step 2.** In the second column, write down the event that caught your attention. Do this as close in time to the event as possible in order to capture the essence of what happened as it occurred.
- **Step 3.** In the third column, write out what this meant to you. (If you have time then, great; otherwise return to record your reflections at a later point in the day.)
- **Step 4.** In the final column, write out what you might do differently or what new choice you may want to incorporate into your life because of the event. Beginning with the word *because* can help to go below the surface.

**Figure 3.1**   Template for a Reflective Journal

| Date | What was said, done, or experienced | This means to me... | What will I now do? |
|---|---|---|---|
|  |  |  |  |

Keeping a journal and stopping periodically to use structured processes can help you to reflect on your own learning experiences in the past as a student, your philosophies presently as a teacher and leader, and your anticipated goals and wants for the future. In this way, you nurture your own integrity and authenticity—the ways you live and work that are congruent with your beliefs about children, about learning, and about the essential purposes that drive the work you do in schools.

# 4

# Inside Connections

## Commitment and Collaboration

CHAPTER CONTENTS

The "Inside" of Collaboration: Shared Connecting
     Through Shared Sensemaking
Congeniality Versus Collegiality in the
     Collaborative School
Characteristics of School Learning Communities
A Case In Point: Sunnyside Middle School
Focus for Reflection, Exploration, and Action:
     Group Learning

Being a part of a group is natural to humans, and collaborating in order to remain in the group or community is equally natural. Belonging is a basic need for all humans (Maslow, 1970).

Nevertheless, effective collaboration takes commitment and a coordinated effort that emerges from understanding collaborative processes from the inside out. We examine collaboration in three ways: (1) by exploring the "inside" of effective collaboration and collegiality that produces that elegant and seemingly effortless process that we see in some schools; (2) by examining what collaboration looks like from the "outside" and the structure and conditions that support authentic collaborative processes; and (3) by describing genuine collaboration in the workplace.

## The "Inside" of Collaboration: Shared Connecting Through Shared Sensemaking

How do people learn and grow collectively? We know that individuals learn through information and experiences in their personal and professional lives. People might dismiss the information and experiences or they might choose to process, discuss, or explore the information and experiences. For example, a teacher attends a workshop and hears a description of direct instruction that includes discussion with other workshop participants and a videotaped observation of that approach in a fourth-grade classroom. The teacher builds that process into lesson plans that are developed in concert with colleagues who also attended the workshop. She then tries the approach and modifies the procedures based on her own assessment, student responsiveness, and feedback from a colleague who observes her. Had this teacher dismissed the lecture and observation, any learning about direct instruction may have been unused and forgotten. Instead, this teacher processed information individually and with another to enhance her learning and practice in direct instruction. Such learning is both individual and social. We make sense of information and events in our own experience both through individual processing and through making meaning in social contexts (Bandura, 1986; Weick, 1995).

Individual sensemaking leads to collective sensemaking in professional organizations. In fact, individuals rarely make sense by themselves of organizational events and actions. Rather, sense is made through dialogue and exchange of ideas, beliefs, assumptions, and solutions or actions. Thus sensemaking is the product of people interactively interpreting, sharing, and refining information and experiences. Because we do not have direct access to each other's knowledge, experience, and thoughts, we achieve shared understanding through communication (Rasmussen, 2001). We communicate ideas through language or actions, and the receiving persons interpret the communication through their own knowledge experience and thoughts. In the social context of schools, one person's understanding is a product of his or her own construction of meaning around the communicated ideas. Fully understanding each other's points of view may require many communicative exchanges. Hence, dialogue and sharing the same psychological and physical space over time is a critical element in collective sensemaking.

Although we know much about how individuals learn, we know considerably less about how groups learn. We assume that group learning is accomplished through the individual learning of group members, but we know that the result transcends a compilation of an individual's learning, producing a whole that is greater than the sum of its parts (Fauske & Raybould, 2005; Senge et al., 2000). When group members learn from shared experiences, they begin to develop similar knowledge, assumptions, beliefs, values, and emotions that guide their behaviors and actions (DiBella & Nevis, 1998; Fauske & Raybould, 2005; Jih & Neeves, 1992). Just as individuals try to "make sense" of information and experiences in their own lives, groups can collectively make sense of shared information and experiences.

People making sense of their environment collectively are central to the collaborative experience. People try to create order in and to "make sense" of their lives by connecting events as sequential or causal or, when no sense can be made, as divine or serendipitous. When an uncle dies of lung cancer after forty years of smoking, relatives are saddened but can make sense of his death. When a child dies from cancer, parents may say it was an act of God, but few can make sense of such a tragedy. Making sense becomes making peace with oneself—an endeavor at times hard won.

Sensemaking pervades and defines much of what we do as a member of a group or an organization (Weick, 1995). Members of an organization try to impose order and sequence to the tasks and events of their work. They explore and analyze power and influence, organizational imperatives for action, and who really has a voice and who is respected and "heard" in negotiations. In education, sensemaking often centers on questions regarding our students. Which students are performing well and why? What is the cause of the achievement gaps that exist? How can we best work together to improve student learning? What practices can we adopt to improve instructions? How can we effectively engage parents and the community to support student learning? What are the achievement goals for this year and will we meet them? How can we raise the reading scores of these challenged third graders or help these ninth graders in transitioning to high school? People project, predict, and plan their work. Indeed, individually and collectively, educators continually approach professional settings and endeavors through a sensemaking lens that helps make their work both doable and understandable.

*In my fifth year as a middle school language arts teacher, the school district where I worked made a commitment to shift to the teaching of "writing as a process." Funds were provided for members of the language arts department to attend workshops and conferences, to take courses, and to meet together to share approaches and strategies. My own first attempts, after several years of teaching mostly from the grammar book, led to classroom management issues when I withdrew old structures and asked my students to spend their time writing. But in meetings with members of my department, I learned how other teachers were organizing writing folders, received examples of mini-lessons others were teaching, participated in developing writing rubrics together, and eventually even had opportunities to share samples of my students' writing, critiquing these and the work of other teachers' students to establish a common set of exemplars for various genres of writing. These interactions with colleagues provided the foundation that I needed to "institutionalize" this new approach within my own classroom without any ongoing management problems, even in the face of my principal's comment ten minutes into my formal observation that year that "the form I am using doesn't fit the way you are teaching!"*

Not all shared experiences and information are received and retained in exactly the same way for all members, but when enough elements are the same, shared language and understanding emerge across group members. The kind of learning is supported by consistent patterns, goals, and leadership. It is this shared sensemaking that occurs in collaboration and results in emergent, shared goals and shared language that bind organizational members together as a community.

## CONGENIALITY VERSUS COLLEGIALITY IN THE COLLABORATIVE SCHOOL

While the very basic human need for belonging to and participating in a group is met by schools that are congenial, truly collaborative schools move from being congenial to being collegial (Barth, 1990). Consider the congenial school:

*The principal is friendly and laid back, often away from the school visiting the district office. He is well liked by the superintendent as well as the teachers and building staff. Teachers readily congregate in the lounge before and after school and frequently meet off school grounds to socialize. Teachers enjoy the latitude that they have in lesson plans and testing. The halls are filled with discussions of football games, homecoming, and other extracurricular activities. Parents are meeting in the library to organize Booster Club activities for homecoming week. The cheerleaders and several football players are in the lunchroom hanging decorations. The school mascot and team members are displayed prominently and the team lockers are decorated. Students talk happily in the halls, and the faint sounds of the band practicing drift past. Teachers here meet in departments about once per month to coordinate the pace of moving through the content assigned to each grade. Guidance counselors also meet together to coordinate scholarship applications for seniors as well as support for applications to college. Overall, the school is a happy and pleasant place to work and study.*

Collegiality, on the other hand, requires the presence of four specific behaviors. The adults in collegial schools

1. Talk about practice in conversations that are frequent, continuous, concrete, and precise;

2. Observe each other engaged in the practice of teaching and administration;

3. Engage together in work on curriculum by planning, designing, researching, and evaluating curriculum; and

4. Teach each other what they know about teaching, learning, and leading (Little, 1981, as cited in Barth, 1990, p. 31).

Now consider a collegial school.

*The principal and the assistant principal sit in a meeting with the instructional team consisting of nine elected representatives from each department. Along with the principal and the assistant principals, each of the team members will observe teachers and offer training when requested in the areas that they have been trained as trainers. They are planning professional development activities for the rest of the year. The teachers' lounge is the meeting spot for a group of teachers who are planning a field trip for the ninth- and tenth-grade earth and physical science classes. Student government is meeting in the lunchroom to organize the next session of freshman orientation and mentoring. One group of guidance counselors is reviewing the midterm referrals from teachers of students who are in danger of failing. Another group is planning the next standardized testing session and the afterschool study sessions for those who want extra help. The main office display cases showcase winning entries into the state one-act play competition. The homecoming schedule is posted with the upcoming week's activities, including times before and after school for decorating lockers and the auditorium pep rally. Parent volunteers are assisting with Internet research in the media center. The halls are buzzing with talk of senior projects, graduation portfolios, and the homecoming football game. Energy is high.*

Congeniality can depict a situation where people cooperate and are respectful and cordial to each other. Pleasantness and lack of conflict prevail. People are accommodating to others' beliefs, and they allow for each other's individuality and freedom of expression. All of these factors are important to maintaining a comfortable workplace and positive outlook. However, our work is not always comfortable nor should it be. In fact, discomfort or disequilibrium is exactly what produces learning (Piaget, 1991). It is only when we experience disequilibrium that we make adjustments or accommodations our thinking in response to assimilating new information. In this sense, conflicting approaches, ideologies, and values can precipitate learning under the right circumstances. Lack of disequilibrium, in fact, can cause people as well as whole organizations to become stale and stagnate. The congenial school, while a pleasant place to work, can promote mediocrity by consistently failing to push staff and administrators to think reflectively about their work and to disagree or decide among tough choices. Conversely, a collegial school encourages collective reflection on practice and open discussion of choices—a setting where examining one's work is expected routinely, new ideas and risk taking are encouraged, and there is a focus on shared purposes. This process includes deeper, "inner" learning and shared, "outer" learning (Fullan, 1993) that can reshape a school and redirect its resources and energy through true collegiality as a school learning community.

## CHARACTERISTICS OF SCHOOL LEARNING COMMUNITIES

Authentic engagement and openness can be learned through individuals sharing their practice and developing a culture and community of inquiry. Sometimes called professional learning communities (PLCs), these dynamic, collegial cultures share several characteristics (DuFour & Eaker, 1998; Hord, 1997; Louis & Kruse, 1995; Waters & Cameron, 2006), shown in Figure 4.1.

**Figure 4.1**   Characteristics of School Learning Communities

1. Educators across the school share values, vision, collective efficacy, and language that focus on student success.

2. A culture of creativity, inquiry, and openness to new ideas is actively nurtured and shared through ongoing dialogue.

3. Genuine and authentic participation in agreed upon processes by school community are embraced by all.

4. Multiple opportunities, structures, and recognition for reflection and dialogue exist across the school.

5. School leaders at all levels consistently in directing energy and resources toward achieving results.

Source:   (DuFour & Eaker, 1998; Hord, 1997; Louis & Kruse, 1995; Waters & Cameron, 2006)

These five characteristics, when sustained over time, are indicative of a dynamic and purposeful school community that has the capacity and the will for ongoing examination and refinement of instruction focused on student success. Unity of purpose with commensurate clarity of vision and language develops from educators interacting in multiple ways to garner and direct their energy and resources toward explicit and measurable goals. Fear of risk taking diminishes; openness and trust prevail to allow introspection and self-disclosure. Asking for help is valued and giving help is commonplace. Encouraging collaboration among teachers through the concept of study groups (Murphy, 1999) illustrates this process. The following describes one school's experience.

During a recent school year, a local school district implemented a system for thirty additional hours of collaborative learning in all schools. At one middle school, this was translated into a rich elaboration of the school's existing structure of PLCs. A development committee including the principal, the school's literacy coach, and the school's data coach, along with a representative of each interdisciplinary team was responsible for developing group learning experiences, defining criteria for good classroom assessment and good common assessments, and identifying criteria for effective instruction.

Whole faculty study sessions were held on Tuesday mornings with a focus on classroom assessment. Thursday mornings, grade-level subject area groups called PLCs met to process and apply their learning from the Tuesday morning sessions. In addition, one meeting a week of interdisciplinary teams looked at cross-curricular implications of the new assessment learning of teachers across subject areas. The purposes of these meetings were multiple:

- to develop a common language about assessment and a set of shared purposes across subject areas within the team;

- to create good structures for team meetings to help teachers make more effective cross-disciplinary connections;
- to make explicit cross-discipline shared language and classroom assessment practices;
- to focus on cross-disciplinary connections essential to the FCAT, Florida's statewide assessment; and
- to field-test cross-disciplinary tools such as a writing rubric and short and long response question formats.

Once a month, whole department meetings were held by each subject area group to work through issues of policy and practice emerging from the various learning experiences. For example, the math department determined it was important for them not only to act on but also to engage colleagues in other departments in implementing their shared belief that reading decimal numbers correctly will help students understand decimal numeration. They declared, "As math teachers, we will consciously try to always read decimal numbers correctly—4.7 will be read 'four and seven tenths.' We will refrain from reading 4.7 as 'four point seven.'"

Toward the end of the year, teachers identified common themes:

"What's working:

- core department meetings are useful for taking whole faculty learning and tailoring it to our needs;
- we like seeing what other schools are doing;
- the work of Tuesday whole faculty study groups makes us look in our Thursday PLCs at things we need to change;
- we are together more as a faculty, and we love bouncing ideas together; [and]
- we like assigned times to do this work and being compensated for it!"

Teachers also raised issues that were substantive and important, clearly geared to improvement not only of the process but also of their own emerging classroom assessment processes. They thought that an hour was too short and caused them to lose track of the information between sessions. They also desired more models of assessment practices and examples from schools with similar demographics to their school. They wondered what data could be used for subjects such as science and social science where state data was not available. They liked the book discussions but wanted more information about the ways that validity and reliability related to their own classroom assessments.

The importance of continued dialogue among teachers and staff, as well as a continual effort to make sense of the work of others and how one's own work is interdependent, frames collaborative school communities (Clark et al., 1996). These characteristics highlight a school community of commitment, respect, and authentic engagement—not merely an outer façade but genuine collaboration.

A façade of collaboration with inauthentic engagement, on the other hand, can lead to inappropriate uses of the structures for control, perpetuation of the status quo, and even collusion (Anderson, 1998; Pounder, 1999). A litmus test of four questions can help assess whether the appearance of collaboration represents genuine and authentic participation: (1) Who participates? (2) In what spheres do they participate? (3) Participation toward what ends? (4) What conditions and processes should be present (Lipman, 1997, p. 29)? When the participants include those who are affected by the decisions and work of the collaborators, and when they have authority, skills, and resources to complete the work, then authentic collaboration is more likely to occur. Over time, these patterns of participation and conditions for success create a community of learners, willing to take risks and genuinely engage—collaborating wide open. Thus authentic collaboration is supported from within through structures and conditions that encourage ongoing and authentic participation of its members by creating norms, rules, and patterns of interaction.

School leaders can foster authentic collaboration and can shift the focus and culture of schools (Boyd, 1996; Fauske,

1999). Successful school leaders of authentic collaboration exhibit specific behaviors:

- They intentionally and knowledgeably create conditions and opportunities that invite collaboration.
- They actively restructure how educators and other participants think about decision making, curriculum planning, and related issues.
- They consciously build communities around shared values.
- They intentionally share responsibility for education with all stakeholders.
- They view their role as facilitators of others and act on the belief that all stakeholders share the goal of quality education for students (Boyd, 1996).

Thus effective school leaders are authentically engaged in collaboration themselves and are not fearful of shared power and collaborative decision-making. Consider the following example of the evolution of teaming in a middle school. To what extent are the elements of collaborative professional community just described present in this example?

## A CASE IN POINT: SUNNYSIDE MIDDLE SCHOOL

The Sunnyside Middle School seventh-grade team was meeting in the team leader's room for its regularly scheduled Wednesday afternoon session on curriculum integration. Deborah had been surprised and flattered to be elected team leader, and she took the job seriously. The principal had asked teachers about four years ago if they were interested in a team model of decision making with emphasis on certain aspects of teaching and learning. The principal and six teachers including Deborah had received district support to attend two workshops on effective teaming strategies and organization. These teachers came back to the school with ideas for organizing teams and for determining the work of the teams. They reported to the other teachers at the monthly faculty meeting and received a positive response. Several teachers wanted to know more. Twelve teachers and the principal visited another school to explore the teaming process on the morning of a staff development day. In the afternoon, the teachers brainstormed a draft proposal for teaming at Sunnyside that was shared with the entire staff for response. The proposal was refined and in the following faculty meeting teachers in the sixth and eighth grades reached consensus for piloting teams in those grades. The eighth-grade teachers were skeptical and wanted to stick with the department structure. Because department meetings included teachers from all grade levels, this became an obstacle to schoolwide implementation of teams. The principal suggested that a committee of teachers from all three grades be formed to discuss the advantages and disadvantages of teaming and what might be lost if the department meeting structure was changed. The principal encouraged those who voiced concerns to be on the committee and had asked Deborah to lead the discussion.

Over the next four weeks, Deborah held two meetings. The first meeting seemed a little disorganized and people were talking about all kinds of issues or advantages for teaming. Deborah decided to let the members speak out rather than try to have a set agenda. When she wrote out the minutes, however, she noticed patterns in the dialogue. The eighth-grade representatives were concerned about preparing students to enter high school and wanted a smooth articulation of students to the ninth grade. They focused on academic preparation and planning for the transition. The sixth-grade teachers were worried about receiving students from feeder elementary schools and had been visiting with counselors at the elementary schools, noting students with special needs. The seventh-grade teachers, however, had been involved with thematic units of study that guided the content and activities for students across social studies, science, math, and language arts. Also the seventh-grade teachers had been meeting in small groups in addition to the regular department meetings because integrating the curriculum required extra time on the part of the teachers. To them, organizing into teams seemed like yet another meeting to attend. Deborah recalled that the teams she had visited earlier in the year were able to focus on integrating the curriculum across subjects. They had also mentioned coordination with feeder and receiver schools. In the minutes, she highlighted the themes that captured teachers' interests and concerns. In the second meeting, Deborah proposed a grade-level team structure that incorporated the seventh-grade teachers' emphasis of thematic units across different subjects. Other teachers on the committee had been trying these units on a smaller scale as well. It seemed that the teachers valued the student learning outcomes associated with thematic units. She also suggested that teachers set aside time for team meeting with feeder and receiver schools and for addressing transition of students, both individual students and groups. The teachers on the committee were unanimously supportive of the plan, but were skeptical about how much time it would take. They were reluctant to move forward with the proposal unless there was some way of providing meeting time besides before and after school. The principal was not a member of the committee, and Deborah was nominated to ask the principal about the time for meetings. The principal pondered ways to make time for teachers to meet regularly and went to the district with a plan to lengthen each school day by twenty minutes, allowing students to be dismissed early on Wednesdays. The district administrators were not generally receptive, but the associate superintendent over curriculum, new to the district, spoke in favor of the plan. She had been in a district where middle school teams had been adopted. She offered some advice for implementing the plan: (a) involve the parent organization in the planning, and (b) hold community "town meetings" to explain that the plan was not reducing instructional time, but rather allowing teachers to address student needs more systematically. She also suggested providing a parent- or volunteer-staffed afterschool program on Wednesdays for students whose parents could not provide supervision. With the districts and the principal's support, the teachers decided to try teaming for at least one year. Several months later, I observed several team meetings in my study of teaming practices and noted some substantive patterns of authentic engagement and dialogue about individual as well as teamwide practice. In the final twenty minutes of one team meeting, a teacher of three years reported on the progress of a student who was struggling with reading and writing. The teacher had described this student to the team and asked for ideas for academic improvement.

Admitting that one needs help and taking the risk to ask for help are clear signs of healthy dialogue in a professional community of practice. The teachers at Sunnyside had developed a system for monitoring student progress that can help them make sound instructional decisions. They have found, however, that the progress monitoring system is extremely helpful in offering a profile of the student but less helpful in knowing how to respond instructionally. They devote a portion of team meeting time to dialogue about instructional responses to student data. In developing this monitoring system, the teachers had also developed a PLC and had begun to weave a seamless plan for addressing the needs of students. This school had begun to emerge as a PLC where the shared and consistent focus was on student learning with an ongoing dialogue about instructional improvement with teachers authentically engaged and not afraid to take risks—collaborating wide open.

Thus collaboration is based on shared experiences and interpretations among people who are working toward a collective goal. The degree of commitment to the collaborative process is directly related to the extent that the collective goal satisfies individual needs or goals of group members. The implicit assumption is that groups who collaborate well can learn and grow professionally as a group as well as individually; a mutually adaptive and beneficial relationship thrives. Thus genuine collaboration has the potential to promote growth and change for individuals as well as groups and organizations. As collaborators, they not only plan, decide, and act jointly, but they also *think together,* combining independent conceptual themes to create original frameworks.

Also in a true collaboration, there is a commitment to shared resources, power, and talent: no individual's point of view dominates, authority for decisions and actions resides in the groups, and work products represent a blending of all participants' contributions (John-Steiner, Weber, & Minnis, 1998, p. 149). Authentic collegiality enhances the collaborative relationship to a high level of caring and mutual nurturing that, in turn, can augment collaboration. Not surprisingly, we collaborate well when authentically committed to shared goals in a situation where collaboration and collegiality are valued, expected, and consistent. Collaboration happens around shared goals that in schools are sometimes refined by educators but are mostly predetermined by many elements in the school setting. Conditions, structures, and related supports can enhance collegiality and the success of collaborative efforts, but ultimately, ongoing success emerges from trusting, open relationships.

## FOCUS FOR REFLECTION, EXPLORATION, AND ACTION: GROUP LEARNING

Authentic collegiality and collaboration occurs most often in groups that are a subset of the whole organization. Especially when your school is large, your personal opportunities may be limited to such a subset group.

Study groups can provide an opportunity for authentic collaboration and can allow both new and experienced teachers to examine, compare, and refine practice. Study groups can take a variety of forms from simply meeting regularly to discuss an article or a book about new strategies to meeting each week with a focus on student achievement data and appropriate responses from teachers. Sometimes study groups emerge as a vital structure in schools and are supported by hiring substitutes or alternative means of releasing teachers to participate in what is viewed as essential work.

When teachers meet on a regular basis to voice their concerns, dilemmas, or successes with teaching and learning, they begin to develop a shared language and understanding of teaching practices. They can resolve issues and solve problems by deprivitizing practice for receiving feedback according to the focus of different types of study groups. These kinds of small group activities show exceptional promise for positively influencing teaching and learning (DuFour, 2002; Murphy, 1999). Changes in teaching practice often are seen within a few months' time and flourish as the study group continues. Study groups require thoughtful planning and a focus on curriculum, teaching, and student learning is key to study group organization. Authentic engagement in study groups leads to collaboration and collegiality that, in turn, can nurture each of us professional and create a community of learners in schools.

For example, consider a high school faculty that is collectively concerned about the struggles that students are having with lack of study habits and skills. The department chairs explored the possibility of training a few teachers in various subject areas to become experts on study skills and to train other teachers. Starting with a few volunteers who were sent for a series of professional development training activities, the school supported a cadre of five faculty members to become experts. These five faculty members trained about twenty additional members of a faculty of 115 in the first year. At the end of the year, the faculty set a goal of training 85 percent of the teachers over the next two years. Ultimately, the department chairs implemented a system in third year in which one member of the department who had become a trainer was given an extra release period that was devoted to modeling, coaching, and supporting other teachers' development of expertise in using study skills to help students learn. The one extra release period in this large high school meant that class sizes were increased by one to three students—a price that the faculty felt was minimal given the positive schoolwide impact on student learning.

Group learning focuses the attention of teachers and leaders on issues of shared concern in schools. What is or might be the place of group learning in your own school environment?

1. Do you participate in study groups in your school? Reflect on the last time you were engaged both collegially and collaboratively in your professional environment.

2. Take a moment to record your feelings, the nature of interaction, the purpose of the work, and the outcomes, both in terms of products and relationships.

3. Think about the cultural characteristics of the workplace, assessing the support available for collaboration, recognition for your work, valuing of relationships, and resources available to support the effort.

4. What experiences would you like to continue or revive?

5. How can you begin a regular dialogue with other professionals about new ideas and strategies? In what ways might you engage others in exploring new ideas, undertaking a joint inquiry, or engaging together in the study of a professional book? Who is most open to collaborating with you in these ways?

Your responses to these questions provide the context for the next steps you can take to enrich, expand, or initiate group learning in your own setting. Learning together with likeminded colleagues can be an important component of making a difference for students in a variety of ways including advocating change in schools, which is explored in the next chapter.

# 5

# Outside Actions
## Agency, Efficacy, and Advocacy

Many schools commit to the importance of having adults in schools who know students by name, monitor their progress, and communicate with parents or guardians. Small learning communities, class size reduction measures, and related "school within a school" efforts all aim at creating a space where students are positively connected to adults in the school setting. Programs based on "communities of caring" or character building have similar purposes. The notion of advocacy for children by educators and parents is becoming more common and expected.

Some educators maintain that parents and community constituencies have been hindered from advocating for certain populations of students. They cite the growing social divide between teachers and the families of many of their students that produces frustration and feelings of powerlessness for both groups (Hargreaves, 2001). When teachers feel that their purposes and integrity are threatened, they distance themselves even further from the parents through word and action, blaming parents for lack of concern and criticizing them for poor or negligent parenting (Hargreaves, 2001, p. 1067). Parents conversely characterize schools and teachers as "not in touch" with the real world, at least as defined by the background of the parent. The gap between community constituencies and schools reflects these same patterns and perceptions. Hargreaves observed, "Teaching has become an occupation with a feminine caring ethic that is trapped within a rationalized and bureaucratic structure" (p. 1069). He noted that teachers have distanced themselves from students and their families in numerous ways and categorizes many levels of emotional misunderstanding, stereotyping, and masking of honest reactions on the part of teachers. A kind of pervasive emotional disingenuousness has emerged to replace the seamless networks of schools and homes that many communities enjoyed earlier in the twentieth century. Rather than advocating for the child together and with similar purposes and shared understanding, teachers and parents often are not attuned to cultural differences and may work at contrary purposes, confounding the efforts of both. Teachers advocating in their own ways for students may inadvertently disregard family or cultural norms, fears, or expectations. Parents advocating for their children may do so with little regard for the school as an institution or the teacher as an extension of that institution.

# THE INVESTMENT OF "EMOTIONAL LABOR"

Hargreaves (2001) cited examples in which parents lie to school representatives to protect the student and observed that such an act may be considered acceptable or even admirable when that institution has failed the parent or others in the families. For example, parents who have kept their students out of school for family reasons, either because the parent has a day off from work and can spend time with children or because the parent desperately needs an older child to care for a younger sick child to keep that parent from getting fired, can lie to the school to protect both themselves and their child from retribution. Hargreaves cited these and other instances of cultural incongruence between families, communities, and teachers as demanding "emotional labor" from all stakeholders (p. 1070).

The "emotional labor" of maintaining relationships by masking true feelings or positions can exact a high personal and professional cost (Hargreaves, 2001, p. 1073). On one hand, the ability to manage one's emotions is viewed positively as professional competence (Goleman, 1995); on the other hand, it can be viewed as masking our emotions and undermining our self-efficacy (Hochschild, as cited in Hargreaves, 2001). Subordinating one's own feelings and beliefs is described as "sacrificial, exploitative, and unauthentic" (Hargreaves, 2001, p. 1073). Alternatively, the act of temporarily subordinating feelings and beliefs in such a way as to maintain respectfulness and opportunities for future communication ultimately has the potential to be rewarding. Thus emotional labor can be either fulfilling or exploitative according to power relationships and purposes at stake in the workplace (Hargreaves, 2001, p. 1073).

## SELF-EFFICACY

The interpretation of whether emotional labor is fulfilling or draining has much to do with one's level of self-efficacy, belief in our own competence and in the value of the work that we do. The concept of self-efficacy is based on the relationship between three factors: personal factors (including cognition and emotion), behavioral factors, and environmental factors (Maddux, 1995). Self-efficacy represents one's own view of individual capabilities enhanced or hindered by the ability to creatively garner environmental resources and choose among various actions wisely. Do we perceive ourselves as effective and powerful in our environment? In other words, self-efficacy is an assessment of our own competence and the resulting mental model that then guides our actions. In relation to emotional labor, self-efficacy is a critical determinant of our perceptions of fulfillment versus exploitation.

*At one point when I was teaching seventh- and eighth-grade English language arts, some teachers with very strong opinions joined our group, and before long, the expectation became that the taught curriculum would focus almost exclusively on the grammar book—the red book for seventh grade and the green book for eighth grade—with three weeks of writing instruction being "allowed" at the end of the year. At first, I thought that perhaps because I was not as comfortable teaching grammar as these other teachers, I was not feeling good about the new thrust. Even after taking a professional development course offered for colleagues by one of these teachers on the finer points of grammar, my unease continued. As the second year of this "regime" began, in my eighth-grade classes, I had students I'd taught the year before in seventh grade, as well as students who had had the grammar-only proponents. I noticed that only a small portion of the grammar-only students had retained the key points of the grammar instruction from the year before. At about that same time, I attended a workshop with Julia Thomason of Appalachian State University and learned that only about 20 percent of eighth graders can consistently reason abstractly about abstract material. I knew I needed to blend the teaching of grammar with applications as part of ongoing, year-long experiences with writing. I attended workshops and courses on how to effectively teach writing as a process, and developed professional relationships with colleagues outside my school that had expertise in teaching writing. The following year I went against the decision of the group and let my students choose: "Shall we wait until the end of the year to do some writing, as most of the other classes will do, or shall we spread the writing instruction throughout the year?" The students chose to spread the writing throughout the year. As a result, both the students and I had a more effective and fulfilling experience. I explained the thinking behind the decision to the group at my school but was not successful in convincing them to follow my lead. I consequently moved to another school where my thinking was more aligned with fellow writing teachers, a place where the teaching of grammar and mechanics was embedded in ongoing writing experiences.*

When we feel hopeless to change things, we may experience the subordination of our views and feelings as draining or, in extreme cases, exploitative. Conversely, if we believe that we are capable and can make things happen, then we may be more likely to subordinate our feelings temporarily in order to achieve a greater purpose. Sometimes we may be compelled to overcome feelings of helplessness to develop avenues for advocating for students as well as for ourselves— to nurture our own self-efficacy.

## AGENCY

Self-efficacy is tied to perceptions of power or powerlessness and our opportunities for agency—belief in our ability to change the environment. To a large extent, the ability to change the environment emerges from a parallel ability to manage resources and influence people. We know people who behave very differently within the same environment. One person sees a mistake as a failure and retreats; another sees a mistake as a minor setback and simply makes a different step or choice. Similarly, some colleagues are more influential among their peers than are others, and the perceived ability to influence others emerges from deeply held feelings of self-efficacy.

> *In the late 1980s and early 1990s, there were teachers in Vermont middle schools in and near Chittenden County who were dissatisfied with things as they were. Working in departmentalized settings or on four-person "interdisciplinary" teams that were mostly teams in name only, these teachers dared to dream of something different and better. Meeting each other in the first courses and institutes offered in the state focused on middle-level education, taught by Chris Stevenson of the University of Vermont, these teachers banded together to explore the possibility of smaller, more truly integrated teams. Calling themselves "Rebels WITH a Cause," they met monthly for several years, often for dinner meetings over pizza or salad. Though the Alpha Program at Shelburne Middle School, mentioned earlier, had been around for many years, teacher Carol Smith acted as a cheerleader, mentor, and coach to colleagues who aspired to create something better in other schools. Soon, "Blaze" and "Pride" were born at Camels Hump Middle School. "Odyssey" began at Essex Middle School. And so it went as innovative teams took root in the midst of the more conventional programs in their respective schools. Years later, these teams or their descendents are still in operation, and many have been studied to learn the benefits they offer (Bishop & Allen-Malley, 2004).*

Although some changes are readily accepted, even to unanticipated levels as in the example just mentioned, other attempts at change may produce conflict. Ponder a situation in which teachers started a single, stand-alone gifted program in a separate location from the various schools where it originally had been housed. The teachers strongly resisted the new superintendent's move to phase out the program and again redefine it as a school-based program with greater access to all students, especially students of color (Conway & Calzi, 1995, p. 3). A principal was appointed to oversee the transition of the program. The roles of these teachers would change to consultants and resource teachers, and they would be relocated to various schools. These teachers not only resisted the principal's attempts at change, they also aroused parents to voice resistance and subsequently wreaked havoc in the district. This example illustrates how well-meaning teachers can come in conflict with equally well-meaning administrators; educators acting on differing conceptions of what is best for students. These incidents raise several important questions with regard to agency:

1. How do we balance conflicting individual or small group goals?

2. How do we treat the unequal status among participants groups?

3. What place does advocacy for a particular cause or position have in collaboration?

Some tension among people and goals competing for scarce resources is a natural and desirable state. The teachers acting to best serve their immediate students had negative consequences for other students. The superintendent and principal created disequilibrium (rocked the boat) and, in the positive sense, pushed these teachers to reexamine their earlier decisions and encouraged thoughtful change. By using influence in this way, an educational leader may not be considered an "equal" to teachers in the collaborative process. Similarly, influential parents, community leaders, politicians, and businesspeople can have uneven levels of influence on decision-making processes. Yet all of these stakeholders can share central values and beliefs about student learning.

Engaging in collegial and professional agency as a leader or a teacher does not necessitate abandonment of roles, duties,

beliefs, and perspectives. The mistaken belief that collaborative processes require that all members have equal status can
create a mind-set in group culture that leaves no space for
leadership other than that which emerges from the group
(Conway & Calzi, 1995; Wildalsky, 1989). Recall the conceptu-
alization of *and* in relation to multiple roles (Atkinson, 2001);
one can be both a follower *and* a leader, an insider *and* an out-
sider. Being an agent for change does require honesty and
transparency of participation and underlying motivation. One
does not abandon beliefs or values but rather one takes a
respectful and thoughtful stance and openly advocates from
that perspective, exercising agency for change. Others' views
are similarly expressed and, ideally, a collaborative decision
or solution emerges from the dialogue.

In addition, when educators are delegated authority to
establish programs, it is a very natural and desirable tendency
to feel commitment to these programs. Difficulty can arise
when ownership of those programs causes educators to
extend their prerogatives and power beyond the completion
of the task assigned. Agreeing upon the tasks, realm of authority, and term limits of collaborative efforts at the outset can
avert confusion later (Conway & Calzi, 1995). Clarity of task,
purpose, and length of participation keeps us honest, and
honesty fosters trust. Thus stakeholders with differing status
and perspectives and who are advocating different approaches
can share overriding and compelling goals that can sustain
collegial relationships and processes.

## Advocacy Revisited

To advocate is to become engaged, to learn what needs to
be done for the benefit of children, individually or collectively,
and then to do "it," to ask for "it," or to make "it" happen.
One's capacity for advocacy emerges from all that defines us
personally and professionally from the inside out. It flows
from deeply held mental models, beliefs, assumptions, values,

and norms, explored in Chapter 4 that guide our actions and interactions with others as full professional participants and change agents. Where there is congruity among our various selves and where we can comfortably live the multiple roles of *and*, such advocacy allows us at once to take a stand while engaging honestly and authentically with colleagues—true to ourselves, respectful of others, while openly espousing a cause or protecting a concern.

*Growing up in the Deep South provided several opportunities to receive instruction from, work with, and report to African American female educators who were extremely competent and impressive. Some were teachers of mine in high school: an AP English teacher was remarkable in her knowledge and ability to inspire and motivate students, and a chemistry teacher who was rigorous, thorough, and caring in her superb chemistry instruction. Others were teachers in the predominantly African American schools where I taught and some were mentors to me. Pearl Braxton, professor of reading, was extraordinarily reflective about her experience as an African American female educator and about the impact of school integration on young African American students. She described her experience in the segregated schools that she had attended and the relationship of teachers on those schools to their students, particularly those of color, and allowed me to understand, within in the limits of my own experience and race (Caucasian), the passion with which many of these teachers approached the classroom. They were wholly committed to student learning and held high the expectations and aspirations that all students can learn and achieve. As we learned to trust one another, she allowed for me a glimpse of the commitment and strength that she brought to her work, and sense of responsibility and advocacy for students. The schools that she and other African American young people had attended were located in neighborhoods where people knew each other by name. One's history teacher might be a relative or attend the same church. Faces were known around town and anonymity was next to impossible. The principal was well known and respected; a word to your parents would produce an immediate response. Teachers knew each other well and communicated about individual students' successes and failures. While such a close-knit community could be burdensome and meddlesome at times, it also created a seamless safety net for many students, a village of support. My colleague lamented the lack of similar support for African American students who seemed to get lost in the White schools, or at least did not experience the same level of scrutiny or support. She believed that such commitment to success for students of color had been compromised in the immediacy of integration and hoped that over time, the rigor and high expectations for all students would reemerge.*

In many ways, the school community that my colleague described here is similar to the various current efforts to develop PLCs and supportive structures in schools. *Students were connected to adults in these schools, and caring adults acted as their guardians and mentors.*

In PLCs, advocating for all students is the essential work of teachers and leaders and is a means for creating a seamless support system that is socially just and inclusive. As adapted from Marshall & Gerstl-Pepin (2005), leadership advocacy in education (which she referred to as social justice advocacy leadership) blends several different leadership theories/change models. These suggest a set of self-assessment questions that can be used to reflect upon our own efficacy, agency, and advocacy as teachers and leaders:

- Critical pluralists advocate democratic participation:
  - To what extent are children and teachers in our classrooms/school/district engaged in democratic processes in relation to decisions and plans that impact their lives?
- Transformative approaches recognize oppression and engage in dialogue for change:

- – Who is excluded from important decision-making processes in our classrooms and schools? Why is this so? What needs to change?
- – What forums are needed for dialogue regarding issues of equity?

- Moral and ethical approaches nurture and develop children for the good of the whole:
  - – How are demands of accountability balanced with opportunities to respond to individual needs?

- Feminist "caring" approaches develop inclusive, facilitative relationships between and among school, families, and community:
  - – In what ways might families and the community better be involved in two-way processes of communication, inquiry, decision making, and action?

- Spiritual/cultural approaches support networking and coalition building (Marshall & Gerstl-Pepin, 2005, pp. 270–272):
  - – Who are the key individuals and organizations that share a similar commitment to the education and success of all students? How might they best collectively exercise their commitment?

Educators who advocate, then, are those who "ensure participation, act ethically, transform inequitable relations, care for the individuals they lead [and teach], and value cultural differences" (Marshall & Gerstl-Pepin, 2005, p. 271). Advocacy can also afford the opportunity to more broadly influence schools, teachers, and students by influencing the social and political structures and people in decision-making positions. Influencing policy decisions at the local, state, and national levels is both a responsibility and an obligation for educators.

*I was working as a consultant to a school districtwide project in which teacher leaders were trained to facilitate the work of curriculum development committees for all subject areas. For one school year, all inservice days were dedicated to this project with the expectation that nearly final drafts would be shared with the appropriate curriculum specialist at the state's Department of Education. In March, the Chair of the Math Committee sent off the draft, only to receive critical feedback indicating the developmental scope and sequence the group had adopted was not acceptable; they needed a grade level by grade level scope and sequence instead. At that time, the state's Public School Approval Standards required that curriculum include a scope and sequence, but there was no requirement that it be organized by grade levels instead of a developmental progression. The state's math expert had overstepped his role in imposing a philosophy rather than upholding a regulation.*

*As it happened, the following week a statewide professional development conference took place that was attended by principals and a large number of the curriculum directors in the state. When I raised the issue with them, they decided to create a position paper and send it to the Manager of the Curriculum and Instruction Division of the state's Department of Education. Amazingly, two meetings were held in a very short period of time, and the paper was completed just two weeks later. The Manager met with the group and recommended a joint task force to create a document that would be a tool to support school districts in developing high quality scope and sequence documents based on any one of several well-researched approaches. And back in the school district, the math committee was able to finish their draft and focus their energies on the task of beginning implementation.*

A more radical approach to initiating social changes on behalf of oppressed or underserved populations is offered in Alinsky's (1989) *Rules for Radicals* as tactics for living with each other and dealing with the world. Although we cannot fully embrace Alinsky's tactics because they include ridicule and disrespect as mainstays of subversion, the passion and intelligence of his views have spawned many followers who have taken at least a few of the strategies for change to heart, particularly his zeal for nurturing all persons to make sense of their lives in a way that produces order and allows them to thrive. His admonition to laugh and to enjoy the "fight, and to kindle the passion of living creativity" ring true in relation to the themes and concepts of this book. Authentic passion for a cause and patient, caring pursuit of one's passion can indeed evoke change.

## COMMUNICATION

When educators advocate improving schools for the benefit of students but fail to develop and implement an effective communication plan to engage parents and the community in the process, they are frequently met with numerous reactions and challenges. Depending on the level of trust among the stakeholders, these questions can run the gamut from clarification or natural curiosity to skepticism, cynicism, and outright opposition (Ledell, 1994). In fact, for any improvement or change effort, a rule of thumb is that 15 percent of the public will meet the change with easy acceptance, 70 percent will need convincing, and 15 percent will opt for rejection (Doyen & Scattergood, 1995). According to Ledell (as cited in Cushman, 1993), a former school board member and a consultant on issues of communication with communities,

> The choice is between developing a communications strategy upfront or going back to retrofit one later. You pay now or you pay later. And everybody knows it's more expensive to retrofit something than to design it right from the start. (pp. 2–3)

Planning and carrying out good processes and communications can facilitate change efforts in schools. Suggestions for effective communication between school leaders and community constituencies anticipate and avoid potential pitfalls:

- Don't take things personally. Treat all stakeholders with openness and respect.

- Don't repeat or try to disprove unsubstantiated assertions.
- Use simple, straightforward language.
- Provide press releases to the media.
- Seek expert advice and legal counsel when necessary.
- Identify a point person to respond to questions.
- Work to identify common ground (Doyen & Scattergood, 1995; Ledell, 1994).

Time spent planning up front often pales in comparison to the time and the damage that could result from faulty communication or if those who need to be involved are not engaged from the outset. When difficulties do arise and stakeholders confront each other, then using principles of skillful negotiation is essential. Four principles can help in negotiating with opposing individuals or groups (Fisher & Ury, 1983):

1. Separate people and issues. Doing so allows the parties involved to deal with the issues without damaging their relationship.

2. Focus on interests, not on positions. Often backing up from positions to interests allows for the identification of common interests from which new, shared positions can be generated.

3. Generate options for consideration.

4. Use objective criteria for choosing the best decision and resolving differences. Determine these criteria prior to starting the work to resolve the disagreement.

Using strategies such as these, teachers and leaders can effectively bring those on the outside into the conversation about improving schools for the benefit of students. Thus teachers and school leaders can build bridges for advocacy that bring parents and other community stakeholders into the communication spiral, making them "insiders" to an authentic and trusting school environment.

*As codirector of a state's standards development project when I received a call asking if I would be willing to review and critique a videotape made by parents about standards. These parents had recently served on their local school's Standards Task Force, and they believed that others on the committee and in the community did not understand the positive impact standards could have if appropriately developed and implemented. One of the parents was the president of one of the largest communications firms in the state; the other was an organizational development consultant. Together they created a short, twenty-minute videotape that traced the journey of students through communication standards from the primary grades through the district's standards-based high school graduation project. The importance of students knowing what they are to learn, the value of teachers sharing a context for teaching and learning, and the benefit of integrating communication standards across the curriculum was clearly illustrated. All these two parents wanted in return was to know that the state's department of education would be willing to copy and distribute the tape to each school in the state.*

This is a clear example of advocacy as a matter of seeing a need and exerting effort to address that need. Whether a teacher in an individual classroom advocating better materials, better curriculum, or more family engagement for students; whether a parent standing up for the needs of his own child; or whether the parents just mentioned using their skills to try to impact the educational system statewide, advocacy is about taking action to effect change.

## FOCUS FOR REFLECTION, EXPLORATION, AND ACTION: ACTION RESEARCH

Action research is a process of inquiry and study of an event, process, or experience that involves the participants and occurs during the unfolding of that event process or experience. Action research works on the assumption that stakeholders whose lives are affected by the focus of study should be the primary investigators (Stringer, 1996). These "stakeholder researchers" go through a process of rigorous inquiring, gathering information, and reflecting on that information in order to come to some understanding of the issues, events, processes, or experiences under study (Stringer, 1996, p. 10). Action research is a hands-on approach to making sense of our experience—reflection on action and in action (Schon, 1983) through rigorous, data-driven inquiry and analysis. Similarly, advocacy is grounded in ongoing practitioner research to identify and examine issues, explore options, make decisions and act to put solutions in place. Action research is a valuable tool for exploring school issues from the inside out.

Educators participate regularly in action research. Every time we teach a lesson and adjust it for the next class based on how it unfolded with the first, we are doing action research. Exploring how other schools have set up a parent volunteer program while in the process of setting up such a program at our own school is action research. This exploration and analysis of "data" in our professional lives is both commonplace and valuable.

To extend your exploration of efficacy, agency, and advocacy, consider conducting a small action research project of your own. For example, if you had an interest in how collaboration plays out, you might identify all of the groups in which you work professionally. Then, you could use structured observation to study how those groups function. Does the group accomplish its goal? Are the voices of all members valued and respected? Do members disagree and discuss alternative views, eventually coming to consensus? In the group that you consider the most collegial and trusting, you might ask the members to explain why they participate and what they hope to gain from participation. Share your own perspectives as well. In a chart, you could then record and compare the responses across group members to determine the degree of congruity between each individual's stated reasons and goals for participation and the unifying purposes of the group's work. If the group is working in a spirit of authentic collaboration, then those individual goals should align well with the group goals. If you conduct the same activity in a group that functions less genuinely and effectively, you will likely find more disparately between individual goals and group goals, and you will find more incongruity between stated purposes and actual outcomes or actions. However, initiating a discussion of this nature in a poorly functioning team can potentially highlight some disparities, help the team recognize incongruities, and provide a vehicle for taking action to adjust the group's interaction and productiveness. If the group is willing and open, you can then collectively set goals, activities, and boundaries for interaction and work.

In considering an action research project focused on your own concerns about areas in need of action in your current work environment, consider those issues of greatest concern to you. For example,

- why do so few parents participate in school activities;
- to what extent are students involved in democratic processes in our classrooms;
- what is the nature and tone of professional discourse among the professionals in this school; and
- in what forms do students receive feedback about their learning?

Filling in the blank questions and stems such as those shown in the following can be useful tools in generating questions to pursue:

- What do students _____ when _____?
  *What do students learn from field experiences in science?*
  *What do students study when given opportunities for independent research?*
- How do other teachers _____ after _____?
  *How do other teachers modify their instruction after analyzing data from classroom assessments?*
  *How do other teachers implement new practices after engaging in professional development?*

- When is the best time to _____?
  *When is the best time to contact parents?*
  *When is the best time to begin a new writing program?*
- Why does/doesn't my use of _____
  _____?
  *Why doesn't my use of open-ended questions elicit useful responses from teachers in post-observation conferences?*
  *Why does my use of individual goal setting with students improve their learning?*

Once your questions are identified, decide whether this is a project that you had best conduct on your own or in concert with some similarly interested colleagues. Then, alone or together, determine the most efficient and effective way to address the question(s). Will you

- conduct a survey
- create and use an observation protocol
- keep a journal or log of your own perceptions or practices
- interview key individuals
- analyze documents
- conduct an Internet or library search for essential resources on your topic of interest?

In choosing the method or approaches you will use, be sure to use the simplest means to gather the data you need most effectively.

Once the data are collected, determine what they tell you. What responds to your initial question? What new questions are raised? Who else needs to know of your findings? What stance or position must you take, given what you have found out? What action will you take because of what you have learned? These new learnings and new questions lead to new inquiry and action, an ongoing cycle of noticing, questioning, exploring, and acting, which in the end are the heart of efficacy, agency, and advocacy.

# 6

# Inside Inspirations

## The Spirit of Teaching and Leading

Most teachers and school leaders begin their careers in education based on a strong desire to make a difference in the lives of children. This belief in one's own ability to have an essential impact is connected to an overarching faith in the power of the positive, an acceptance of one's inherent connection to something larger than one's self, and a worldview that encompasses the importance of service in one's life. Examples of the spiritual nature of our professional lives are always present in our work in schools, whether we acknowledge them or not (A. N. Johnson, 1999).

Yet, some schools have veered sharply away from the initial idealistic leanings of educators who seem collectively to have lost hope. There are even schools in which teachers speak disparagingly of students, the students' parents, and the colleagues with whom they work. That teachers and leaders continue on in these schools, working sometimes year after year in an environment that feels hopeless or even unsafe to them, speaks not just to the intensity of their vocational dilemma but also to the spiritual crisis in which they find themselves. Restoring, protecting, and valuing the spiritual dimensions of our professional work are key to exploring teaching and leading from the inside out. This chapter explores the spirit of teaching and leading by explicating the concepts of spirituality, democratic practice, and sustaining passion for our work.

## SPIRITUAL CONSIDERATIONS FOR TEACHING AND LEADING

Spirituality in education refers to no more—and no less—than a deep connection between student, teacher, and subject—a connection so honest, vital, and vibrant that it cannot help but be intensely relevant. Nourishment of this spark in the classroom allows it to flourish in the world, the arenas of politics, medicine, and engineering—wherever our students go after graduation (Jones, 2005, p. 1).

According to Jones, spirituality in education encompasses four essential dimensions:

- Spirituality as transcendence—going beyond the surface of the subject; learning to see with new eyes;
- Spirituality as connection—the connection of teachers to students, "the students to each other, and everyone to the subject being studied" (Palmer, as cited in Jones, 2005, p. 5);
- Spirituality as wholeness—making room in the classroom for all relationships and all layers of relationship to the subject; and
- Spirituality as compassion—addressing human questions in education and living the questions (Jones, 2005, p. 5).

Making schools places of transcendent experience, connection, wholeness, and compassion is the essence of teaching and leading from the inside out. Educators have opportunities every day to connect from the core of their own spirit with students, peers, parents, and others. The spirit of teaching and leading is manifest in the ways we view learners, deal with curriculum and assessment, influence what our classrooms and schools can become, and appreciate and celebrate the best of what happens there.

To fully capture the spirit of learning in classrooms and schools, it is essential that we view all students as capable learners without limits. But even some of the most committed of us can sometimes catch ourselves limiting the potential of our students, perhaps even unwittingly. Wilhelm (personal communication, 1995), a freelance writer frequently writing on education topics, told of the time he was writing a piece about the Association for the Blind. In preparing to write, he arranged to meet at school a young boy who was blind.

On arriving at the school, he asked the child what the first class would be, and the boy said, "Physical education." "Oh, and what will you be doing in physical education?" Wilhelm asked. "Archery," the child responded nonchalantly, to which

Wilhelm said he inwardly rolled his eyes and thought perhaps this visit would be a waste of his time. But once in the gym where the targets were set up, Wilhelm discovered the boy had been assigned a "coach." Like every other child in the room, the boy was given two arrows. He asked his coach a number of questions before taking aim with his first arrow and shooting, hitting the target just outside the bull's eye ring. He then asked his coach to describe for him where the arrow had hit and what the relationship was of that location to the bull's eye. Taking aim the second time, he hit the bull's eye.

Wilhelm reported that what was particularly striking was that the sighted children in the room took the task far less seriously, and not only did they not hit the bull's eye, but in many cases, they even missed the target! Yet the child who could not see had demonstrated exemplary purpose, focus, and spirit given the task at hand.

Consider a second example of inaccurate perception of student abilities: a middle school student who had multiple physical challenges and was unable to speak. He had little social interaction with other students, who were awkward around him and tended to avoid eye contact. Then, his social studies teacher obtained a voice synthesizer attached to a computer for him. Using this tool for the first time, the boy was able to participate in the class geography bees. It became immediately evident that he had a vast store of knowledge of geography, and soon other children in the class would vie to have him on their team.

Paying attention to the conditions and context of learning, especially for students who have challenges, can significantly impact the opportunities students have to excel and to connect. As well, examining our own assumptions about learners, surfacing any possible limiting assumptions or biases, is critical.

To teach and lead with spirit is to teach and lead from the inside out, creating classrooms and schools that are vibrant places of engaged, meaningful learning for children and adults alike. This takes a deeply personal commitment, a willingness to step forward to make a difference, and a propensity for finding like-minded colleagues with whom to dream and do. Often these connections are made within schools, and sometimes they are made across schools as well.

## IN OR OF A DEMOCRACY? HOW WHO WE ARE INFLUENCES WHAT OUR SCHOOLS BECOME

The spirit of teaching and leading relates to democracy in schools and to democratic life. Many of our schools fall short of providing and valuing expressions democracy for either adults or students. Apple and Beane (1995) in *Democratic Schools* paraphrase John Dewey: "If people are to secure and maintain a democratic way of life, they must have ways to learn what that way of life means and how it might be led" (p. 7). Apple and Beane identified seven characteristics of democratic schools as follows:

- Ideas flow freely, and all involved are fully informed about happenings of concern to them.
- Individuals and groups are regularly involved in finding and solving problems.
- Critical reflection and analysis are used to analyze ideas and reflect on problems.
- The welfare of all and the "common good" are of central concern.
- Dignity and the rights of individuals and minority groups are honored.
- Democracy is not just an ideal to be pursued; it is an idealized set of values to be lived and to guide our lives in school and out.
- Schools and other social institutions need to model and promote democracy as a way of life for adults and children alike.

In democratic classrooms, children have opportunities to choose among options and to help decide the course of their own learning.

*During my primary years, England's educational pendulum went through a cycle of seeking new ways to inspire children to learn through a very child-centered curriculum. One particular school year left an indelible impression on me—to the extent that I now frame much of my constructivist teaching practice and philosophy of how young children best learn based on that experience. I can recall vividly that single year of education. I remember at the beginning of each week having to decide upon numerous options that were available on the large blackboard. During the week, we went about our projects and activities, which consisted of baking, pottery, playing chess, and an assortment of novel projects. We did this mostly unassisted. Years later, when teaching primary grades, my own teaching philosophy mirrored these early years.*

In classrooms and schools where democracy is promoted as a way of life for children and adults alike, choices are abundant. Children of all ages are directly involved in decisions that impact their lives, using agreed upon criteria to assure high-quality choices. It is not a matter of anything goes, but rather an opportunity to focus together on what is important, to share in crafting the learning and teaching environment, and to look together at work produced and critique the work for areas of strength and areas in need of further development.

Effective, democratic, and spiritually focused educators carefully consider the individuality of each student while simultaneously acknowledging high standards of learning and performance that assure substantial development of each student's potential. The ongoing push for greater accountability in the form of tests and commensurate evaluation/ranking of schools, when carefully and thoughtfully administered, can perpetuate the notion of communities sharing responsibility for student learning. When narrowly interpreted, these requirements for accountability can produce blame placing, excuse making, abdicating behaviors, and high-pressure environments that can even get in the way of learning.

The accountability movement is another example of mechanization in the curriculum. Teachers are expected to be constantly testing students so that the public is satisfied with what is going on in the classrooms. Unfortunately, the tests focus on a very limited portion of the curriculum and ignore the important areas such as personal and social development. These tests tend to stress information that will soon be forgotten by the student. The student begins to see school as a game where succeeding is based on passing tests that seem to have no relevance to anything except what we might call useless knowledge. When school is seen as a game, there is no vitality. Classrooms become lifeless places where students focus on achievement in a narrow and competitive manner. A curriculum of meaningless tests is another example of education without soul. (Miller, 1996, p. 4)

Only a few state plans include rich and broad standards that cut across the various subject areas and promote interdisciplinary treatment. Following the call of the National Governors Association in 1989 for the state level development of standards for student learning, all but one states throughout the country began the development of frameworks of standards. In all but two states, Minnesota and Vermont, the standards documents were discipline specific. In Vermont, a Common Core of Learning had recently been adopted that identified three fields of knowledge (arts, language, and literature; history and social sciences; and science, math, and technology) and four areas of vital results (communication, reasoning and problem solving, personal development, and social responsibility; "Vermont Framework," 1989). Commissions were formed to draft the standards for the three fields of knowledge as well as the vital results standards, those standards that applied to all three fields. Of these, the personal development and civic/social responsibility standards are unique in standards documents nationally.

Briefly, the personal development standards include (a) developing worth and personal competence; (b) making healthy developmental and lifestyle choices; (c) making informed decisions for personal success; (d) building relationships for teamwork, conflict resolution, and roles/responsibilities; and (e) workplace skills such as dependability, productivity, and career planning. Civic/social responsibility standards include (a) service to the community and involvement in democratic processes; (b) understanding diversity, cultural expression, and the effects of prejudice; (c) and exploring continuity and change in relation to their local environment and heritage. These kinds of standards underscore for Vermont teachers of prekindergarten through twelfth grade the importance of matters of the spirit.

Students in the Alpha Program, a multiage, grades six to eight team at the Shelburne Community School in Shelburne, Vermont, collect documentation for the vital results standards in learning portfolios.

We begin with Vermont's vital results standards and work backward, constantly showing students how to recognize quality work and make good decisions so they can produce it. Instead of organizing the portfolio by traditional academic subjects, we encourage students to divide their work into the four essential skills identified by the vital results—communication, reasoning and problem solving, personal development, and civic and social responsibility—and a fifth category that we added—functioning independently.

At the end of each trimester, we turn those weekly goals into a progress sheet listing successes and continued challenges, which help frame new goals for the following trimester. Parents and teachers get copies of these reflections and provide additional comments. Then we all come together for student-led conferences, which last from one to three hours each (C. Smith & Myers, 2001).

Artifacts for portfolios and for discussion in the student-led conferences emerge in a learning environment in which the curriculum and pedagogy are student self-directed, holistic, and integrated/interdisciplinary. Using a process adapted from the work of Beane (1993), teachers in the Alpha program engage students in generating questions about themselves and the world as the starting point for the curriculum for the year. Once the two sets of questions are brainstormed, common themes across both sets are identified and then prioritized. Those themes deemed top priorities are then listed in order, and that order becomes the sequence in which the themes are studied during the year. Vital results standards, the field of knowledge standards, and their associated grade-level indicators are then taught and assessed through the most relevant theme(s). Thus the Alpha Program exemplifies many of the characteristics of democratic schools.

Democratic schools also embrace cultural and ethnic differences that shape the lens through which we see the children we teach. The American landscape is changing radically. It is estimated that by 2010, over one-third of children entering our schools will be members of groups currently designated as "minorities" (National Commission on Teaching and America's Future, 1996). The increase in immigration from Eastern European as well as third world countries in South America and Africa now rivals in size the great immigrations of the nineteenth and twentieth centuries. Meanwhile, preservice teachers remain mainly White, female, and 22 with limited experience of people from cultures different from their own (National Commission on Teaching and America's Future, 1996).

These teachers may not be prepared for the unique perspective, cultural norms, and educational experiences that this influx is going to bring. Teachers' response sets are likely limited with regard to the sorts of instructional approaches most effective for students whose culture differs from their own. Such background, ethnicity, and cultural differences dictate a high level of care and competence for schools and teachers that is responsive to and respectful of students and educators.

Although specific programs, methods, and curriculum vary, there are shared factors that define the nature of effective, democratic schools. Meier (2002) captured the spirit of teaching and leading as an endeavor that allows each educator to find his or her own way with equivalent degrees of care and attention to nurturing the growth and development of students. She described the art of living together with difference, of balancing advocacy with respect. Her analogy of her garden as compared to other gardens demonstrates how one person's interpretation can differ and one can be tempted to say, "You are wrong" or "Do it my way." She preferred wild and unplanned planting beds while others prefer manicured, formal plantings (pp. 175–177). Either is acceptable and even beautiful though very different, and both require constant care and vigilance. Similarly, effective, democratic schools can manifest many forms, but the unifying, shared factors are passion for and commitment to colleagues, students, and their families—to preserving the spirit of teaching and leading.

## TEACHING AND LEADING AS MORAL AND LOVING ACTS

Sergiovanni (1999) focused on moral leadership as a form of transformational leadership that focuses on building a caring and supportive community of learners. The values that educators bring to they work clearly reflect passion and even love for students and each other as well as their work. Yet he observed that educators generally are not comfortable talking about their roles and especially leadership in such "sentimental" terms (Sergiovanni, 1999, p. 91). We continue using old language and paradigms associated with management and function. This language constrains the fullest and most efficacious development of teacher leaders' and school leaders' passion for their profession that goes well beyond descriptors of strategies, curriculum, and accountability:

The essence of teaching lies beyond surviving in the classroom, beyond classroom management concerns, beyond curriculum content and process, and even beyond the developmental needs of students. [It] results from simply understanding students with the mind and heart—it is an act of love. (Bergstrom, as cited in Stevenson & Carr, 1993, p. 1)

Using the metaphor of love rather than power and authority frees us to imagine possibilities because our capacity for love is infinite while our capacity for power is generally viewed as finite; if we give some away, we have less. When we shift paradigms to conceptualizing power in the same way that we conceptualize love, we can begin to envision the possibilities of engendering our own power and efficacy as a means of engendering the same in others. Indeed, a spiral of strength and empowerment—and yes, passion and love—becomes the conduit for integrating our professional selves with shared moral purposes:

> Moral action implies some level of initiation, of personal choosing, of a person willing to engage others for purposes beyond "need fulfillment." In one sense, moral action implies self-fulfillment, but not in some narcissistic concentration on isolated self-gratification. Rather, it is a fulfillment of the self through involvement with an authentic participation in a community's struggle to become more humane, more just, more compassionate, more loving, and yes, more productive, in the sense of making the world a healthier, safer place where the goods of the earth are shared more fairly than they are presently. (Sergiovanni & Starratt, 1988, p. 91)

We can highlight the spiritual dimension juxtaposed against the role of advocacy through Meier's (2002) lens of "democratic habits of mind." We are teachers and leaders who can model democratic practices, assuming responsibility and authority for the success of our schools in a way that values and nurtures our student while also modeling advocacy, taking on authority, when it impedes doing what is best for teaching and learning. The multiple dimensions and forms of teacher leadership and school leadership allow us at once to be critical *and* transforming *and* moral *and* ethical *and* spiritual *and* caring. Indeed, it is the ultimate expression of *and*.

## Focus for Reflection, Exploration, and Action: Making Curricular Connections

The activity offered here differs from most of those offered in other chapters in its outward focus—actively building a democratic culture in schools. Students' questions about themselves, their communities, and the world provide rich sources of curriculum (Beane, 1993), as do students' interests and hobbies outside of school. These can be elicited from young children through individual conferences or group discussion. Valuable information can be gathered from older students by having them individually complete the student questionnaire shown in Figure 6.1.

The same open-ended starter questions can be used to have students identify questions about a topic of study that has already been identified by a textbook or curriculum guide within any subject area. Teachers in teams or grade-level groups can compare common themes that emerge.

Sometimes it is helpful before asking students to complete the survey to have them "warm up" by focusing on themselves. You might say, "Begin thinking about yourself. Who are you? What are you like? What are your interests? What questions do you have about the world?" You might have them jot down a few thoughts before you give them the questionnaire. Also you might want to model the types of questions you would like them to generate (e.g., Why does the moon go down? How do penguins survive in the cold? What is the process for getting a book published?)

After collecting the student surveys, analyze them for common issues and concerns. Are there questions that are repeated by several students? Do you see common themes? What potential topics of study do these suggest? How can these be used to make connections across the curriculum?

**Figure 6.1**   Student Questionnaire

This questionnaire is designed to gather information about your questions about yourself, your community, and your world. Please respond three times to each question starter on the left of the chart—once for questions you have about yourself, once for questions you have about your community, and once for questions you have about the world. If you need more room to write, please feel free to write on the back of this sheet.

| Questions I Have | About Myself | About My Community | About the World |
|---|---|---|---|
| How can I _____? | | | |
| When will _____? | | | |
| I wonder if _____? | | | |
| I wish I knew why _____? | | | |
| I wish I knew more about _____? | | | |
| I wish I knew when _____? | | | |
| Interests: What are your hobbies and interests outside of school? | | | |

This activity illustrates the essential connection between schools and their students. It is through these and related genuinely inclusive approaches that teachers and leaders can begin to build democratically grounded learning communities in schools, thus making them more deeply responsive to the spirit of the adults and children who work and learn there.

# 7

# Outside Perspectives

## Professional Appreciation and Celebration

$W$e see much in the media about what is wrong with schools. At times, it seems almost human nature to focus on what is wrong rather than on what is right. Oddly, this is particularly true within schools, where the same teachers who give frequent positive feedback to students too often remain silent about or critical of their own accomplishments and those of colleagues (Evans, 1996). The common failure to recognize and acknowledge good practices has become a part of school culture:

> A complex pattern of norms, attitudes, beliefs, behaviors, values, ceremonies, traditions, and myths that are deeply ingrained in the very core of the organization. It is the historically transmitted pattern of meaning that wields astonishing power in shaping what people think and how they act....And all school cultures are incredibly resistant to change, which makes school improvement from within or from without—usually so futile. (Barth, 2002, pp. 6–7)

These astonishingly powerful historical patterns and perspectives pervade the extended school community with far-reaching sociopolitical effects.

*When I meet a noneducator and tell them I work as a consultant in education, frequently the response I receive is something like, "I wish you could work with our schools. Schools are in deep trouble." When I ask, "How long has it been since you've spent a full day in a school?" the typical, sheepish response is some iteration of "not for a long time." I invite the person to visit any school and see the good things that are happening. I explain that a benefit of my work, working in leadership development and systems development in schools and districts, is that I get to meet teachers and principals all over the country who are committed to doing good things for students and to doing what it takes to help young people succeed. I get to see firsthand those strategies that work, the incredible commitment of adults to students, and the joy of students achieving their dreams. I also get to see the confounding conditions, limited resources, and trying social and political contexts in which these dedicated educators work.*

Yet, it is increasingly evident that a focus on positive images of the future plays a significant role in countering negative images, beliefs, and expectations.

> The more an organization experiments with the affirmative mode, the more its affirmative...competence will grow. This is why, in many organizations that have experimented with it, people have come to believe that organizationwide affirmation of the positive future is the single most important act that a system can engage in if its real aim is to bring to fruition a new and better future. (Cooperrider, 2000, Para. 8)

Affirming shared beliefs, values, and purposes about improving student learning can motivate and give life to the school community.

The old adage admonishing us to "walk a mile" in the other person's shoes before passing judgment is certainly apropos to schools and their staffs and faculties. Yet we have not fully explored and identified what factors sustain educators in their challenging work. In this chapter, we flesh out some of those factors and characteristics that sustain the positive energy in schools. To focus on appreciation and celebration is not to ignore real issues that exist in schools but, rather, is to use a different lens to examine schools and consider changes that will benefit students and educators alike.

## RECOGNIZING AND SHARING SUCCESSES

Focusing on the positive can have a tremendous impact even in very difficult times. The power of emphasizing the positive is seen in many venues:

> There have been many studies in the field of athletics that prove focusing on what an athlete did well and imaging the best outcomes have greatly increased results over comparator groups that review mistakes.

Medicine is focusing on the study of health in addition to the study of pathology. (Hinrichs, 2002, p. 3)

Human potential for surviving and thriving in the face of severe trials and challenges is regularly found around the world. Individual acts of bravery and endurance abound: people stranded at sea for days or months, people surviving in jungles to escape persecution and death, or a young brother saving his baby sister from a house fire. Consider the example of Charlotte County, Florida, where half the schools in the county were destroyed in 2004 by Hurricane Charley.

*In the fall of 2004, I was working with teachers who were part of a master's degree program in Educational Leadership. All of them were from Charlotte and DeSoto Counties, and when Hurricane Charley hit Florida, four of the fifteen students in the class lost their homes entirely in the storm, and others experienced significant damage to their properties. We agreed to delay the start of the fall semester class by two weeks to try to accommodate these needs, and largely expecting many of the teachers might not continue in the program. Not only did all fifteen continue that semester, but in an amazing display of perseverance and spirit, all those who had lost their homes completed the entire program on time and graduated with the peers in their cohort group. Two students were taken in for a few weeks by other cohort members, and two others moved in with family or friends. When asked how they had continued in the face of such great personal loss, they responded with statements such as, "The house doesn't matter. It can be replaced. I am simply happy to be alive, to have all of my family with me, to have a new appreciation for the colleagues who have helped me get through this."*

By focusing on what was necessary, moving forward to what was positive, and needed by the students and the teachers with whom they worked, the Charlotte County School District was able to stay on track, despite what initially appeared to be insurmountable odds.

Immediately after the storm, it was the voice of the superintendent Dave Gayler that became the source of information via radio each day during the lengthy time before power was restored in the community. Within weeks, schools were back in session with students and teachers from separate schools sharing space within the remaining schools on a split session schedule. Despite the difficulties and the upheavals, test scores in the district had gone up by the end of the first year. Fifteen months later, 16,900 students returned to portable campuses on their destroyed schools' sites (Scott, 2006). Two years later, schools had been rebuilt and were up and running as usual. We saw firsthand the kind of camaraderie, commitment, and spirit that had sustained these educators and those from neighboring districts also devastated by the hurricane. In aftermath of Hurricane Charley in South Florida, the focus on the positive was not only individual, but also organizational. Dave Gayler might well be deemed a "fire starter" (StuderGroup, 2007).

A fire starter is a person who keeps the true essence of the organization alive and flourishing. Fire starters ignite the flame that guides and supports the organization. In early civilization fire was essential to life. People used fires to keep warm, cook food, light the way in darkness, and as a protection from enemies. Without fire people would perish. Within each village (or organization) there were people whose primary job was to keep the fire burning. They taught others how to carry on the practice of keeping the flame burning, which allowed villages to prosper and grow.

The StuderGroup, an organizational consulting and coaching organization founded by Quint Studer to support organizational development in hospitals, promotes stories of "fire starters" who are changing the way hospitals and other medical organizations work today. Essentially, fire starters are "positive deviants" (Whitney & Trosten-Bloom, 2003), people who create positive results without additional resources where others have failed to do so. Whitney and Trosten-Bloom described a study reported in the *Harvard Business Review* about an initiative of Save the Children to reduce childhood malnutrition in rural villages in Vietnam. The consultants found mothers whose children were not malnourished and discovered that these mothers fed their children three or four times a day rather than the usual two times daily. Using an appreciative inquiry approach (Cooperrider, 2000), the consultants "launched a program—delivered by the villagers themselves—to demonstrate to their peers what they had discovered."

Some of the mothers who deviated from their peers by finding ways to keep their children nourished when most children were malnourished were asked to teach other mothers in the village the strategies they used. Within two years, 80 percent of the children participating in the project were no longer malnourished (Whitney & Trosten-Bloom, 2003, p. 86).

How does the notion of appreciative inquiry play out in schools? Can educators duplicate this pattern of sharing good ideas as a regular practice for ongoing improvement? In schools, it is essential that the success of the fire starters and the helpful discoveries of the positive deviants be acknowledged, recognized, appreciated, and celebrated (Schmoker, 2006).

> The single best lowcost, high leverage way to improve performance, morale, and the climate for change is to dramatically increase the levels of meaningful recognition for—and among—educators . . . Recognition refers to praise or positive feedback, but also to validation, to acknowledging and affirming a truth about a person or situation. (Evans, 1996, p. 254)

To be most effective, recognition should be specific rather than general and should align directly with identified purposes of the school (Evans, 1996) such as improving student performance, implementing more engaging instructional practices, tying classroom assessment more directly to identified learning objectives, and so forth.

*One of my responsibilities as a curriculum director for a kinder-*
*garten through twelfth grade school district was to facilitate the*
*work of the Staff Development Committee, which was charged*
*with creating a three-year staff development plan to support*
*implementation of newly developed curriculum documents. The*
*group was struggling to find ways to make the daylong inser-*
*vice days at the start of the school year have more meaning when*
*a seventh-grade science teacher commented, "There is no such*
*thing as a stolen idea." From this emerged "A Celebration of*
*Stolen Ideas," which was a daylong conference offered entirely*
*by educators in the district for educators in the district. The day*
*began with a keynote delivered by the Superintendent, a well-*
*liked, humorous, and very effective speaker. The keynote was fol-*
*lowed by three workshop blocks, each featuring eight sessions*
*from which to choose. Twenty-four workshops were offered by*
*teachers and principals that day, and the evaluation comments*
*about the day were overwhelmingly positive.*
    *"We have a lot of talent in this district."*
    *"This was the best inservice day we have ever had in this*
*district!"*
    *"We should do this every year."*

Specifically, Schmoker (2006) suggested in *Results Now,*
"The key is to be on the lookout for any legitimate effort or
accomplishment that supports better teaching and learning"
(p. 148). Who is the teacher whose students all met the standard
of expected achievement on the recent state math assessment?
Which classrooms have the lowest absentee rates in the school?
To what do these teachers attribute their success? How can
other teachers be involved in observing that teacher modeling
those practices? How can those practices be implemented with
fidelity in other classrooms throughout the school?

## CELEBRATING SMALL WINS

Teachers and leaders work in a context of uncertainty and
unpredictability where external influences can shape their

work, and they must be constantly vigilant about anticipating others' reactions and direction (Fauske & B. L. Johnson, 2001) The sociopolitical context can dictate school goals, and demands for immediate accountability can exacerbate criticism of schools and educators. Still teachers and leaders try to remain focused on their shared values and purposes. In Fullan's (2005) discussion of sustaining school improvement, eight elements are listed as indicators of the potential for real and lasting impact of a change:

1. Public service with a moral purpose

2. Commitment to changing context at all levels

3. Lateral capacity building through networks

4. Intelligent accountability and vertical relationship

5. Deep learning

6. Dual commitment to short-term and long-term goals

7. Cyclical energizing

8. The long lever of leadership (p. 14)

Although all of the elements are applicable to sustaining school change and can be explored further in his book, we focus on only two of those elements here: dual commitment to short-term and long-term goals and cyclical energizing (Fullan, 2005, p. 14). One of the strengths that Fullan noted is the ability to focus on long-term goals with similar commitment and celebration of short-term goals. Instead of waiting to recognize and celebrate completion of the entire strategic plan, for example, he suggested celebrating the small successes along the way. Indeed, he noted that public demands will not allow educators to delay in reporting progress. StuderGroup (2005) offered a similar strategy that they call "quick wins":

> Go for quick wins to establish credibility. A quick win is an action that shows employees you really *are* committed to meeting their needs. If you are trying to

establish an environment of fairness, for instance, don't "pull rank" as a senior leader and cut in line. (para. 4)

Schmoker (2006) took an even more proactive stance by urging educators to intentionally pursue "small wins," then celebrate in order to create momentum and motivation. For example, the first time a group of teachers plans together a lesson focused on an identified skill and all students demonstrate meeting the standard on a miniassessment of that skill, everyone should hear about it. Just as we celebrate the success of the high school basketball teams, and indeed the accomplishments of individual players on the teams, we can celebrate the academic accomplishments and progress of teachers and leaders, highlighting individual accomplishments that lead to team success. Further, just as the coach paces the team and allows time for rest and rejuvenation, the "educational team" needs rest, time to bask in their accomplishments, and space to anticipate the next games and strategies. This "cyclical energizing" (Fullan, 2005, p. 14) is essential for celebrating and sustaining motivation and focus of faculty and staff—pacing ourselves between the "quick wins" while keeping our eye on the play-offs.

## CONTRIBUTING TO THE PROFESSION

Much of the knowledge and skills we bring to our work as teachers and leaders comes from the generosity of individuals in our profession who have shared their wisdom in books and articles, workshops, conference presentations, and courses at universities and colleges. Experienced teacher and leaders have much to contribute to the knowledge base about essential good practices. Individuals learn from each other and the profession, as a whole, advances.

*When I began my career as a middle school language arts teacher, the curriculum was thematic and skills based. Teachers in the department were in the habit of exchanging folders of materials for each theme at the start of every quarter. The teacher who had taught "Mystery and Suspense" one semester would hand off her folder to whomever was teaching it the next time around, knowing she would receive it back for a future marking period with new material included. After several years, the curriculum changed to feature use of a grammar book and a literature anthology, and sharing of materials stopped. Then, one day, I was leafing through old copies of* Learning *magazine, and I came across an article about teachers publishing their own work. I put the article in the mailboxes of several colleagues with a note asking if anyone would be interested in trying to publish one of our units. One colleague responded in the affirmative, and over April vacation, we put together a proposal packet that (not knowing any better) we sent to fourteen publishers. We received thirteen rejections and one acceptance!*

Such work can be celebrated as an indicator of moving forward collectively as a profession, the best work of individuals contributing to the improvement of the professional as a whole.

## ENGAGING IN APPRECIATIVE INQUIRY

How do we identify and plan for the "quick wins" in our schools? How do we build a whole systems approach to positive intervention and change? One method that has shown promise is appreciative inquiry (Watkins & Cooperrider, 2000). Appreciative inquiry is an approach to change grounded in what works, and it assumes that whatever is needed—what is "right"—already exists in the organization. It begins not with a problem that needs to be fixed but instead with a focus on what is working well in the school. Key differences between the problem-solving model and the appreciative inquiry model are shown in Figure 7.1.

**Figure 7.1**    Comparing Two Models

| Problem Solving | Appreciative Inquiry |
|---|---|
| "Felt Need"—Identification of Problem | Appreciating and valuing the best of "What is" |
| Analysis of Causes | Envisioning "What Might Be" |
| Analysis of Possible Solutions | Dialoguing "What Should Be" |
| Action Planning | Innovating "What Will Be" |
| Assumes: Organization is a problem to be solved | Assumes: Organization is a mystery to be embraced |
| Back Door: What is in the way of what you want? | Front Door: What do you want to create? |

SOURCE: (Cooperrider & Whitney, 1999, used with permission)

Because appreciative inquiry starts with the positive, it inherently rallies the energy of teachers and leaders toward their shared central purposes. When we focus on the positive image, we are drawn toward it. After Marotta (personal communication, October 1996), the Superintendent of Schools in West Springfield, Massachusetts, returned from an appreciative inquiry conference in Cape Cod, she was enthusiastic about this model, developed at Case Western Reserve University, and mentioned three aspects as particularly important to her own work in the school district:

1. The importance of beginning with what works

2. The cycle of discovery, dream, design, destiny that guides a systems change process toward what's possible

3. The appreciative inquiry interview process, which she brought to her community as "Celebrating the Stories."

At a time when many schools were engaging teachers in processes of looking at assessment data, identifying where students were not performing well, and planning for change, Marotta requested that the principals of all her schools engage their staffs in processes of analyzing assessment data to identify where students were performing well, hypothesize reasons why they were doing well in those areas, and then plan for how they could do more of what was working.

Subsequently, the first West Springfield Public Schools appreciative inquiry summit was held in September 2002. Four hundred teachers were paid to attend the summit as a professional development opportunity, and they were joined by 100 representative students and about 150 representatives of parents, businesses, and community members. They joined together to "discover moments of greatness, dream about what could be, cocreate possibility statements to guide the whole district toward their dreams, and plan the first step each school could take to start moving in that direction" (Morris, Schiller, Stavros, & Marotta, n.d.).

Appreciative inquiry and "Celebrating the Stories" are not merely about appreciating what is good about our personal work, our interactions with colleagues, or the overall impact of our efforts in schools or districts. Rather, it is an appreciative process leading to action and change based on the best of what is—a process grounded in the following assumptions:

- in every organization, group, or individual something works and can be valued;
- what we focus on becomes the reality we create;
- the language we use creates our reality;
- the act of asking a question begins the change; and
- people have more confidence to journey to the future when they carry forward the best parts of the past (Cooperrider, 2000).

From these assumptions emerged appreciative inquiry's "4D Cycle"—discovery, dream, design, and destiny (Whitney & Trosten-Bloom, 2003):

- **Discovery.** In the dream phase, ideas are gathered about what has worked in the past, what is working in the present, and what are hopes for the future. The heart of this phase is the appreciative inquiry interview, which involves collectively gathering information, sharing stories that emerge from the process, making meaning of themes that emerge. (The last section of this chapter provides guidelines for conducting appreciative inquiry interviews.)

- **Dream.** The dream phase engages participants in using the power of positive images to imagine a better future, in concrete terms.

- **Design.** "Appreciative inquiry design methodology involves people sharing stories of their organization at its best, and then writing statements of their ideal organization. These statements are most often called 'Provocative Propositions.' …At their best, they create an irresistible attraction in the direction of what is described." (Whitney & Trosten-Bloom, 2003, p. 204)

- **Destiny.** The destiny phase involves three related processes: (1) recognizing and celebrating what is already working well or has been changed as a result of the first three steps in the process; (2) using innovation teams to begin action-oriented changes focused on identified goals; and (3) using appreciative inquiry processes throughout the organization in on an ongoing basis.

Excellent examples of tools and processes to use in each phase of the cycle can be found at the appreciative inquiry commons, a site that provides theoretical and practical material and tools for use in many fields, including education (http://appreciativeinquiry.case.edu/).

## FOCUS FOR REFLECTION, EXPLORATION, AND ACTION: APPRECIATIVE INQUIRY INTERVIEWS

The appreciative inquiry interview is a powerful interaction through which stories are shared, connections made, and possibilities presented. While the interview process is often undertaken as part of a broad-scale school redesign process, it also works well as a method of self-reflection or as a shared process between two colleagues or in a relatively small group such as a team or a department in a school.

As a self-reflection opportunity, the following interview questions can be used as prompts from which to write in a journal or log, though there still can be value in sharing with a close colleague any new awareness that emerges. If you choose to use the appreciative inquiry interview process with a colleague or small group, then you can use these examples and suggestions to craft your actual interview questions. These should focus on an "affirmative topic choice," that is, topics are stated in the positive. Thus for example, an interview would focus not on a question such as, "Why are a large percentage of students failing?" but instead on a question such as, "What experiences support our students who get grades of 'A' in their classes?" "What promotes collaboration in our school?" would be a superior question to "Why is the faculty divided?"

Typically, interviews are conducted in pairs, with each person interviewing the other using the same set of questions or interview guide and taking the same amount of time for each interview. In this way, the person being interviewed feels most fully heard. It is important to take notes in order to be able later to share with others the stories and examples that emerge during the interview, as well as to assist in the identification of themes across interviews (where multiple interviews are conducted in a larger group).

Hendrichs reported using the following questions by the Sacred Heart-Griffin School:

1. Describe a time when you were involved in a project or situation where you successfully joined with others to

ensure students were academically, technically, or spiritually prepared for any future. Describe a time that stands out where you felt most alive and most effective. Tell the story.

2. Without being humble, describe what you value most about yourself, your work, and your school community when successful collaboration occurs.

3. Project yourself five years into the future. Sacred Heart-Griffin has been nationally recognized for technological excellence, student academic and spiritual preparedness, and artistic creativity. Changes that began five years ago have been unbelievably successful. Describe what is in place in our school community.

4. What will enable Sacred Heart-Griffin to excel in its mission in the twenty-first century? What is your role in this creation?

To design your own interview questions consider stems such as the following:

1. Describe a time when…

2. Without being humble, describe what you value most about your self, your work, and your school community when…

3. Think of a time when you had a really terrific experience with your school. Tell me the story…

4. Project yourself into the future. Describe what you see in place in your school community with regard to…

5. Please tell me a story about a time when your school (or a book you read) inspired you, your child, or someone you know to become a lifelong learner who continues to be engaged in learning.

Once you have generated the questions and are ready to conduct the interview, find a place where there are no extraneous noises or other distractions. Focus 100 percent on the person being interviewed, following up with probing questions to help clarify the stories being shared. Take notes and, at the end of the interview, summarize the key points of what you have heard. If using the process as a self-assessment in your journal or log, reread your notes from the perspective of someone unfamiliar with the information in them. Is anything missing? Was anything important left out?

When the interview is completed, consider with whom the stories told in the interviews should be shared. If others pairs or teams have engaged in the same process, you could arrange a time to meet with them to identify common themes. Do you and your colleagues have interest in going beyond the discover phase to the dream, design, and destiny phases of the appreciative inquiry change process in order to plan and enact positive change in your school environment? The interview brings to the surface positive aspects of the school as an organization. In so doing, the process provides the opportunity to recognize, appreciate, and celebrate best practices and successes.

# Afterword
## Integrating Our Personal and Professional Selves

**Figure A.1**  Sundance

SUNDANCE
*Dance of Many Colors – Dance of Many Faces*
*The Sun is Outside – The Sun is Inside*
—Yunn Pann

SOURCE: © Yunn Pann, http://www.zisstudio.com and www.ChineseCalligraphyTile.com, used with permission

Integrating our personal and professional selves is a continuous dance, a fluid state of being rather than a set of steps from one defined place to another. Each of us is continually moving and changing, responding in a fluid way to inner commitments and outer expectations; to past experiences, present context, and future hopes; to who we have been, who we are now, and who we have the potential to become in terms of our own individual and collective authenticity, agency, and appreciation. It is a lifelong journey of discovery. The interconnectedness of our professional and personal lives continues even past our retirement years, as we are excited still to recognize our influence on those whom we have taught and led, recognizing the symbiotic nature of influence by passing on the ideas of those who have influenced us.

We began this book with a conceptual framework of teaching and leading from the inside out, a way of thinking about the relationships among the personal and professional aspects of our work, a means of reconnecting with the importance of authenticity, agency, and appreciation. The chapters of *Teaching and Leading from the Inside Out* have expanded on those concepts, going deeper, providing examples, and creating a context in which to consider pertinent issues and implications they hold for the work we do together in schools. It is useful to examine these concepts separately as represented in the following chart, to revisit their meanings, and to consider the potential each has for our work and our lives.

**Figure A.2**   Teaching and Leading from the Inside Out

| Teaching and Leading From the Inside Out | | | |
|---|---|---|---|
| **Inside** | **Authenticity** | **Agency** | **Appreciation** |
| **Personal** | Honesty<br>Integrity<br>Commitment<br>Knowledge of Self<br>Introspection<br>Efficacy | Efficacy<br>Empowerment<br>Ethics<br>Self-Actualization<br>Clear Boundaries | Acceptance of Self<br>Well-Being<br>Maturity |
| **Professional** | Currency in Skills and Attitudes<br>Relational Competence<br>Passion for Work<br>Commitment | Mentoring and Being Mentored<br>Influencing<br>Assertiveness<br>Creating and Applying Theory and Policies<br>Advocacy | Sharing Recognition<br>Celebrating Accomplishments<br>Publishing and Presenting<br>Professional Service<br>**Outside** |

Our "inside out" work takes us in an emergent direction rather than to a "be all end all" stopping point of attainment. Our "inside outness" and our "outside inness" are matched sides of a continuous spiral through which we revisit over time several of these key ideas.

We teach and lead from who we are, how we see our worlds, and how we view ourselves in our worlds. In integrating our personal and professional selves, we strive to be transparent, to recognize our blind spots or shadows, and to acknowledge the interplay between our inner and outer worlds. In so doing, the use of narrative stories helps us to recognize and represent the complexity of the two worlds.

Authenticity and integrity are the essence of the moral purpose of schools, a purpose to which we each recommit regularly and repeatedly over time. Crucial to this recommitment is continually reflecting on who we are, how we work, and the extent to which we are able to respond to the needs of the learners we serve. Reflection is that gift we give ourselves. Through reflection we can ponder, explore, and develop the alignment of our inner selves with our outer expressions of self in professional and personal environments.

Change in classrooms and schools is a continuous, developmental process of empowerment, efficacy, and agency. Integrating our personal and professional selves requires teaching and leading against the grain and being willing to take a stand and to honor the importance of reciprocity of influence (Fauske & B. L. Johnson, 2000, p. 114)—the essential notion that not only are we influenced by our school environment but also that we have the ability and the obligation to actively and intentionally influence that environment and create opportunities that will lead to improved experience and learning for students. We can be effective agents of change.

Learning and teaching are the heart and spirit of the educational enterprise in a democracy. In democratic schools, students, teachers, leaders, and community members engage collaboratively in making the decisions that affect their work together toward the shared purpose of assuring that all students have the opportunities they need to be successful in school and in life.

Collegiality is a learned process of sustained relationship with collaborative others. As coauthors writing this book, we have opened our hearts to each other, challenged our intellect, and shared our essences with each other, both professionally and personally. We enhanced and sustained our connections with one another through the multiple processes of creativity and challenge that are the reality of writing a book. Sometimes the process required that we search out the best in each other and in ourselves.

Searching out the "goodness" in the system allows us to appreciate "what is" and to use that as inspiration for what "could be." Inside out is an ongoing process of lifelong learning; we all have strengths and areas to improve upon—looking inwardly and seeking feedback can be highly supportive in our teaching and leading; the stories of our lives are important. Our personal work and our professional selves wind back and forth in a constant spiral of personal and professional growth.

*I was teaching a graduate course on standards-based curriculum in the school district where I had once taught. One of the students was a former colleague, whom I'll call Jane, from a different school in the district who many years before had commuted with me to the first graduate curriculum course I had ever taken. In the ensuing years, she had remained in her fourth-grade classroom while I returned to the university to earn master's and doctoral degrees, worked as a curriculum director, and ultimately become a consultant and a college professor. During those years, I had also done significant personal development work around issues that I had related to childhood hospitalizations and trauma. Through that, I had learned to begin each day facing the sunrise, raising my arms in a large "V" shape, and celebrating being open to the possibilities of the day, but about this, I had said nothing about this during the graduate course I was teaching. At the end of the last day of the class, Jane came up to me and said, "I so fondly remember our drives together to Montpelier years ago. I am amazed how much you've learned since then, and (raising her arms into a large "V"), I just love how you are with us." After my initially astonishment at the spontaneous replication of the "V," I was delighted to have reconnected with a colleague in this meaningful way.*

In the end, integrating our personal and professional selves is a matter of patience, persistence, and professionalism. We each *do* have what it takes. The essence of teaching and leading from the inside out is the whole in which authenticity, agency, and appreciation are brought together—the best of each teacher's own practice, the heart of each leader's finest work.

# References

Alinsky, S. (1989). *Rules for radicals: A pragmatic primer for realistic radicals.* New York: Vintage Books.

Anderson, G. (1998). Toward authentic participation: Deconstructing the discourses of participatory reforms in education. *American Education Research Journal, 35*(4), 571–603.

Apple, J., & Beane, J. A. (1995). *Democratic schools.* Alexandria, VA: Association for Supervision and Curriculum Development.

Arbinger Institute. (2002). *Leadership and self deception: Getting out of the box.* San Francisco: Berrett-Koehler.

Atkinson, E. (2001). Deconstructing boundaries: Out on the inside? *International Journal of Qualitative Studies in Education, 14, 3.*

Ausubel, D. P. (1967). *Learning theory and classroom practice.* Toronto, Ontario, Canada: The Ontario Institute for Studies in Education.

Bandura, A. (1986). *Social foundations of thought and action: A social cognitive theory.* Saddle River, NJ: Prentice Hall.

Barth, R. S. (1990). *Improving schools from within: Teachers, parents, and principals can make a difference.* San Francisco: Jossey-Bass.

Beane, J. A. (1993). *A middle school curriculum: From rhetoric to reality* (Rev. ed.). Columbus, OH: National Middle School Association.

Bergstrom, K. (1993). Unpublished journal entry. In C. Stevenson & J. Carr (Eds.), *Integrated studies in the middle grades: Dancing through walls* (Introduction). New York: Teachers College Press.

Bishop, P., & Allen-Malley, M. (2004). *The power of two: Partner teams in action.* Columbus, OH: National Middle School Association.

Boyd, W. (1996). *Competing models of schools and communities: The struggle to reframe and reinvent their relationships.* Philadelphia: Mid-Atlantic Laboratory for Student Success. (ERIC Document Reproduction Service No. ED 419 858).

Bramson, R. (1988). *Coping with difficult people.* New York: Ballantine.

Carr, J. (1993). I'm not as smart as I used to be. *Vamle Journal.*

Carusetta, E., & Cranton, P. (2005). Nurturing authenticity: A conversation with teachers. *Teaching in Higher Education, 10*(3), 285–287.

Clance, P. R., & Imes, S. A. (1978, Fall). The imposter phenomenon in high achieving women. *Dynamics and Therapeutic Intervention Psychotherapy: Theory, Research, and Practice, 15*, 1.

Clark, C., Moss, P., Goering, S., Herter, R., Lamar, B. Leonard, D., et al. (1996). Collaboration as dialogue: Teachers and researchers engaged in conversation and professional development. *American Education Research Journal, 33*(1), 193–231.

Cochran-Smith, M., & Lytle, S. (1993). Inside/outside teacher researcher and knowledge. New York: Teachers College Press.

Conway, J. A., & Calzi, F. (1995). The dark side of shared decision making. *Educational Leadership, 53*, 45–49.

Cooperrider, D. L. (2000). Positive image, positive action: The affirmative basis of organizing. In D. L. Cooperrider, P. F. Sorensen, T. F. Yaeger, & D. Whitney (Eds.), *Appreciative inquiry: An emerging direction for organization development.* Chicago: Stipes Publishing.

Covey, S. (1992). *The 7 habits of highly effective people.* New York: Simon and Schuster.

Cushman, K. (1993, May). Essential collaborators: Parents, school, and community. *Horace, 9*(5). Retrieved February 4, 2006, from http://www.essentialschools.org/cs/resources/view/ces_res/116

DiBella, A., & Nevis, E. (1998). *How organizations learn: An integrated strategy for building learning capacity.* San Francisco: Jossey-Bass.

Doyen, M., & Scattergood, P. (1995). *What to do when controversy strikes.* Paper presented at the annual conference of the Association for Supervision and Curriculum Development.

DuFour, R. (2002, May). The learning-centered principal. *Educational Leadership, 59*(8), 12–18.

DuFour, R., & Eaker, R. (1998). *Professional learning communities at work: Best practices for enhancing student achievement.* Washington, DC: National Education Service.

Evans, R. (2001). *The human side of school change: Reform, resistance, and the real-life problems of innovation.* San Francisco, CA: Jossey-Bass.

Fairhurst, A. M., & Fairhurst, L. L. (1995). *Effective teaching, effective learning: Making the Personality connection in your classroom* (1st ed.). Palo Alto, CA: Davis-Black.

Fauske, J. R., & Johnson, B. L. (2003). Principals respond to the extended school community: Fluidity, alignment, vigilance, and fear. In W. Hoy & C. Miskel (Eds.), *Theory and research in educational administration.* Greenwich, CT: Information Age.

Fauske, J. R., & Raybould, R. (2005, February). Organizational theory in schools. *Journal of Educational Administration, 43*(1), 78–101.

Fauske, J. R. (1999). *Conditions that sustain collaboration and encourage trust.* Paper presented at the University Council of Educational Administration Convention, Minneapolis, MN.

Fine, M. (1994). Working the hyphens: Reinventing self and other in qualitative research. In N. Denzin & Y. Lincoln (Eds.), *Handbook of qualitative research* (70–82). New York: Sage.

Fisher, R., & Ury, W. (1983). *Getting to yes: Negotiating agreement without giving in.* New York: Penguin Books.

Freire, P. (1972). *Pedagogy of the oppressed.* London: Penguin Books.

Fullan, M. (1993). *Change forces: Probing the depths of educational reform.* Bristol, PA: Falmer.

Fullan, M. (2005). *Leadership and sustainability.* Thousand Oaks, CA: Corwin Press.

Gagne, R., & Driscoll, M. (1988). *Essentials of learning for instruction* (2nd ed.). Englewood Cliffs, NJ: Prentice Hall.

Galvin, P., & Fauske, J. (2000). Transaction costs and the structure of interagency collaboratives: Bridging theory and practice. In B. A. Jones (Ed.), *Educational policy in the 21st century.* Charlotte, NC: Information Age.

Gardner, H. (1983). *Frames of mind: The theory of multiple intelligences.* New York: Basic Books.

Gilligan, C. (1982). *In a different voice: Psychological theory and woman's development.* Cambridge, MA: Harvard University Press.

Glenn, W. (2004). Imagine the possibilities: A student-generated unit to inspire creative thought. *The English Journal, 92*(5), 35–47.

Goleman, D. (1995). *Emotional intelligence.* New York: Bantam Books.

Goleman, D., Boyatzis, R., & Mckee, A. (2002). *Primal leadership: Leading to lead with emotional intelligence.* Boston: Harvard Business School Press.

Grennan, K. (1989). The journal in the classroom: A tool for discovery. *Equity and Excellence, 24*(3), 38–40.

Hargreaves, A. (2001). Emotional geographies of teaching. *Teachers College Press, 103*(6), 1056–1080.

Harvey, J. C., & Katz, C. (1985). *If I'm so successful, why do I feel like a fake?* New York: St. Martin's Press.

Hinrichs, G. (2002). *AI in schools: SHG workbook.* Geneseo, IL: Positive Change Corps. Retrieved July 22, 2006, from http://appreciativeinquiry.case.edu/practice/organizationDetail.cfm?coid=2388&sector=25

Hochschild, A. R. (1983). *The managed heart: The commercialization of human feeling.* Berkeley: University of California Press.

Hord, S. (1997). Professional learning communities: What are they and why are they important? *Issues About Change, 6, 1.*

Jih, H. J., & Reeves, T. C. (1992). Mental models: A research focus for interactive learning systems. *Educational Technology Research and Development, 40*(3), 39–53.

Johnson, A. N. (1999). Many ways of understanding and educating spirit. *Classroom Leadership, 2,* 4. Retrieved December 13, 2006, from http://www.ascd.org

John-Steiner, V., Weber, R., & Minnis, M. (1998). The challenge of studying collaboration. *American Education Research Journal, 35*(4), 773–783.

Jones, L. (2005). What does spirituality in education mean? Stumbling toward wholeness. *Journal of College and Character, 1,* 7.

Jung, C. (1969). *Psychology of religion.* Princeton, NJ: Princeton University Press.

Killion, J. (1999, Summer). Journaling. *Journal of Staff Development, 20*(3). Retrieved November 7, 2005, from http://www.nsdc.org/library/publications/jsd/killion203.cfm

Kleinfeld, J., & Yerian, S. (1995). *Gender tails.* New York: Martin Press.

Kouzes, J. M., & Posner, B. Z. (1999). *Leadership challenge.* Berkley, CA: Jossey Bass.

Ledell, M. (1994). *How to create common ground. Democracy, communication, common ground, and policy.* Workshop presentation for the Vermont Middle Grades Initiative.

Lipman, P. (1997). Restructuring in context: A case study of teacher preparation and the dynamics of ideology, race, and power. *American Educational Research Journal, 34*(1), 3–38.

Louis, K. S., & Kruse, S. D. (1995). *Professionalism and community.* Thousand Oaks, CA: Corwin Press.

Maddux, J. E. (Ed.). (1995). *Self-efficacy theory an introduction.* New York: Plenum Press.

Marshall, C., & Gerstl-Pepin, C. (2005). *Reframing educational politics for social justice.* Boston: Pearson.

Marso, R. N., & Pigge, F. L. (1990). *The identification of academic, personal, and affective predictors of student teaching performance.* Paper presented at the Annual Meeting of the Midwestern Educational Research Association, Chicago. (ERIC Document Reproduction Service No. ED 341651)

Maslow, A. (1970). *Motivation and personality.* New York: Harper & Row.

Meier, D. (2002). *In schools we trust.* Boston: Beacon Press.

Miller, J. (1996, November 15). *Education and the soul.* Paper presented at the annual conference of the Association for Moral Education in Ottawa, Ontario, Canada. Retrieved November 7, 2006, from http://members.iinet.net.au/~rstack1/world/papers/Education_Soul.doc

Morris, D., Schiller, M., Stavros, J., & Marotta, S. (n.d.). *Celebrate the stories: West Springfield Public Schools (WSPS) appreciative inquiry summit.* Retrieved September 28, 2006, from http://appreciativeinquiry.case.edu/uploads/WSPS%20Summit%2011-14-02%20(final).doc

Murphy, C. (1999, Spring). Using time for faculty study. *The Journal of Staff Development, 18*(3), 20–24.

Nathan, M. J., Alibali, M. W., & Koedinger, K. R. (2001). *Expert blind spot: When content knowledge and pedagogical content knowledge collide* (Technical Report 00-05). Boulder: University of Colorado.

National Commission on Teaching and America's Future. (1996). *What matters most: Teaching for America's future.* Washington, DC: U.S. Government Printing Office.

Noddings, N. (1991). Stories in dialogue: Caring and interpersonal reasoning. In C. Witherell & N. Noddings (Eds.), *Stories lives tell: Narrative and dialogue in education* (pp. 157–170). New York: Teachers College Press.

Palmer, P. (1998). *The courage to teach: Exploring the inner landscape of a teacher's life.* San Francisco: Jossey-Bass.

Palmer, P. (2000). *Let your life speak to you.* San Francisco: Jossey-Bass.

Palmer, P. (2004). *A hidden wholeness: The journey toward an undivided life: Welcoming the soul and weaving community in a wounded world.* San Francisco: Jossey-Bass.

Piaget, J. (1926). *The language and thought of the child.* London: Routledge.

Piaget, J. (1991). *Toward a logic of meanings.* Hillsdale, NJ: Lawrence Erlbaum Associates.

Polanyi, M. (1966). *The tacit dimension.* New York: Doubleday.

Polanyi, M. (1969). *Knowing and being.* London: Routledge.

Polkinghorne, D. (1988). *Narrative knowing and the human sciences.* Albany: State University of New York Press.

Pounder, D. G. (1999). Teacher teams: Exploring job characteristics and work-related outcomes of work group enhancement. *Educational Administration Quarterly, 33*(3), 317–348.

Quenk, N. (1993). *Beside ourselves: Our hidden personality in everyday life.* Palo Alto, CA: Davis Black.

Rasmussen, J. (2001). The importance of communication in teaching: A systems theory approach to the scaffolding metaphor. *Journal of Curriculum Studies, 33*(5), 569–582.

Reid, J. (1999). The relationship among personality type, coping strategies, and burnout in elementary teachers. *Journal of Psychological Type, 51,* 22–33.

Ring, P. S. (2003). Trust. *Administrative Science Quarterly, 48*(4), 720–722.

Rushton, S., & Smith, R. L. (2006). Teacher of the year award recipients' Myers-Briggs personality profiles: Identifying teacher effectiveness profiles toward improved student outcomes. *Journal of Psychological Types, 4,* 6.

Schelble. R., & Fauske, J. R. (2000). *Role of the principal in implementing teams.* Paper presented at the University Council of Educational Administration Conference, Albuquerque, NM.

Schmoker, M. (2006). *Results now: How we can achieve unprecedented improvements in teaching and learning.* Alexandria, VA: Association for Supervision and Curriculum Development.

Schon, D. A. (1983). *The reflective practitioner.* New York: Basic Books.

Scott, A. (2006, Janaury 8). Schools get ready to rebuild. *Sarasota Herald Tribune.* Retrieved January 12, 2006, from http://www.heraldtribune.com

Sears, S., Kennedy, J., Kaye, J., & Gail, L. (1997). Myers-Briggs personality profiles of prospective educators. *The Journal of Educational Research, 90,* 195–202.

Senge, P. M., Cambron-McCabe, N., Lucas, T., Smith, B., Dutton, J., & Kleiner, A. (2000). *Schools that learn: A fifth discipline fieldbook for educators, parents, and everyone who cares about education.* New York: Doubleday.

Sergiovanni, T. (1999). *Rethinking leadership: A collection of articles.* Thousand Oaks, CA: Corwin Press.

Sergiovanni, T., & Starratt, R. J. (1988). *Supervision: Human perspectives* (4th ed.). New York: McGraw Hill.

Smith, C., & Myers, C. (2001, October). Students take center stage in classroom assessment [Electronic version]. *Middle Ground: The Magazine of Middle Level Education, 5*(2), 10–16.

Smith, L., Skarbek, D., & Hurst, J. (2005). *The passion of teaching dispositions in the schools.* Lanham, MD: Scarecrow Education.

*Sommer, R. (1989). Teaching writing to adults: Strategies and concepts for improving learner performance.* San Francisco: Jossey-Bass.

Stevenson, C., & Carr, J. (1993). Introduction. *Integrated studies in the middle grades: Dancing through walls.* New York: Teachers College Press.

Stone, H., James, D., Parker, A., & Wood, L. (2005). *Report on the Ontario principals' council leadership study: Consortium for research on emotional intelligence in organizations.* Retrieved March 16, 2006, from www.eiconsortium.org

Stringer, E. T. (1996). *Action research: A handbook for practitioners.* Thousand Oaks, CA: SAGE.

StuderGroup. (2005, December 28). *Building an emotional bank account with your employees: Eight ways leaders can save for a rainy day.* Retrieved January 15, 2007, from http://www.studergroup.com/dotCMS/knowledgeAssetDetail?inode=206533

StuderGroup. (2007). *What is a fire starter?* Retrieved January 15, 2007, from http://www.studergroup.com/about_studergroup/firestarter/what_is_fire_starter.dot

Tompkins, G. E. (1991). *Literacy for the 21st century.* Upper Saddle River, NJ: Prentice Hall.

Van Manen, M. (1991). *Researching lived experiences: Human science for an action sensitive pedagogy.* London: The State University of New York.

Vermont Department of Education. (1996). *The Vermont framework of standards and learning opportunities.* Montpelier: Vermont Department of Education.

Vygotsky, L. S. (1978). *Mind in society.* Cambridge, MA: Harvard University.

Waters, T., & Cameron, G. (2006). *The balanced leadership framework: Connecting vision with action.* Littleton, CO: McREL.

Watkins, J. M., & Cooperrider, D. (2000). Appreciative inquiry: A transformative paradigm [Electronic Version]. *OD Practitioner, 32*(1).

Weick, K. E. (1995). *Sensemaking in organizations.* Newbury Park, CA: SAGE.

Wellington, B., & Austin, P. (1996). Orientations to reflective practice. *Educational Research, 38*(3), 307–316.

Wheatley, M. J. (1994). *Leadership and the new science.* San Francisco: Berrett-Koehler.

Whitney, D., & Trosten-Bloom, A. (2003). *The power of appreciative inquiry: A practical guide to positive change.* San Francisco: Berrett-Koehler.

Wildalsky, A. (1989). A cultural theory of leadership. In B. Jones (Ed.), *Leadership and politics: New perspectives in political science.* Lawrence: University of Kansas Press.

Woolfolk, A. (1993). *Educational psychology.* Needham Heights, MA: Allyn & Bacon.

# Index